Right from the Start

BEHAVIORAL INTERVENTION FOR YOUNG CHILDREN WITH AUTISM

TOPICS IN AUTISM

Right from the Start

BEHAVIORAL INTERVENTION FOR YOUNG CHILDREN WITH AUTISM

SANDRA L. HARRIS, PH.D. &
MARY JANE WEISS, PH.D., BCBA

Sandra L. Harris, Ph.D., series editor

Woodbine House ◆ 2007

Published in the United States of America by Woodbine House, Inc., 6510 Bells Mill
Rd., Bethesda, MD 20817. 800-843-7323.

Library of Congress Cataloging-in-Publication Data

Harris, Sandra L.
  Right from the start : behavioral intervention for young children with autism /
Sandra L. Harris and Mary Jane Weiss. -- 2nd ed.
      p. cm. -- (Topics in autism)
  Includes bibliographical references and index.
  ISBN-13: 978-1-890627-80-5
  1. Autistic children--Behavior modification. I. Weiss, Mary Jane. II. Title.
  RJ506.A9H269 2007
  618.92'85882--dc22

                                                                    2006038879

Manufactured in the United States of America

10   9   8   7   6   5   4   3   2   1

In Honor of Our Mothers,

Felice Harris and Joan Rita Coneys,

with love, gratitude, and admiration

And in Celebration of Mothers Everywhere

Who Bring So Much Love and Energy

to Their Children with Autism

Table of Contents

Acknowledgements

This book is the result of our many years of collaboration with one another and with a remarkable group of colleagues at the Douglass Developmental Disabilities Center and the Rutgers Autism Program. We are grateful to Maria Arnold, Marlene Brown, Marlene Cohen, Lara Delmolino Gatley, Lew Gantwerk, Rita Gordon, Jan S. Handleman, Barbara Kristoff, Robert Larue, and Donna Sloan for all they have taught us over many years. Without Jean Burton, professor emeritus in Psychology at Rutgers University, there would not have been a Douglass Center. Generations of children and families owe her thanks.

Parents and children are our most important teachers. To all of the families who have honored us with the care of their children over these many years, we express our deepest thanks for their trust and collaboration in the education of their child. We know there is nothing more precious to a parent than the welfare of a child. We appreciate the contributions of the many families whose advice is found at the end of every chapter in this book. Although they have remained anonymous to protect the privacy of their families, their sharing has enriched this book. We also thank the following people for their contributions to the book: Amanda Harris, Ilona Harris and Gary Zuckerman, Jay E. Harris, Rania Labib, Robert and Cindy LaRue, John and Regina McAllen, Robert Owens, Tina Rivera, Fouzia Samy, Dawn Umemoto, and Shira Yudkowitz.

On a personal note, our thanks to Danny Weiss, who is probably the best psychologist we know! Mary Jane thanks Danny for always being there and for making everything better, and her children for the joy and meaning they bring to each and every day. Mary Jane thanks her mother, Joan Rita Coneys, for her wisdom, courage, loyalty, and love, and her late father and brother for all the love, laughter, and memories. Her thanks also go to her sister, Ruth Anne, her nieces, Lisa and Jessica, and her Aunt Ronnie, as well as to forever friends, Lisa Martin, Ellen Yeagle, Lynne Stern Feiges, and Jacqueline Geoghegan, for their love and support. Sandra thanks her brother, Jay, and sister-in-law, Maxine, for their love; her dear friends, Rhona Leibel and Jean Burton, for support beyond the call of duty; her niece, Ilona, and nephew, Gary, for their loving presence and wisdom; and her grandnieces, Emma and Molly, and grandnephew, Jake, for the joy that comes from the sheer fact of their being.

Introduction

We have written this book to help parents become informed consumers of treatment for their young child with an autism spectrum disorder. Our hope is to educate parents about the reasons that applied behavior analysis is essential in the treatment of every child with autism, and to help them learn how to locate first-rate services for their child.

Since we wrote the first edition of this book (Harris & Weiss, 1998), there have been significant changes in the array of resources available for children on the autism spectrum and their families. A variety of naturalistic teaching methods have become more widely used in educating young children, and many more public schools and early intervention programs are now offering specialized individual instruction or small classes for young children who have a diagnosis on the autism spectrum. It seems important for us to update the first edition of *Right from the Start* with more information about methods that are gaining empirical support and broader acceptance. Although discrete trial teaching remains an important tool in the toolbox, we have added to this second edition an expanded discussion of a broader range of applied behavior analysis (ABA) methods that show great promise in the hands of skilled practitioners.

Another major shift in the field is the growing recognition of the value of the credential as a Board Certified Behavior Analyst or Board Certified Associate Behavior Analyst. Although there are many senior professionals without the BCBA who have worked in the field for a number of years and who offer superb services in

Applied Behavior Analysis, the BCBA credential helps families, programs, and schools identify many other individuals who are well grounded in the principles and practice of ABA. The person holding the BCBA credential may offer direct service, and/or supervise other staff members who are certified as Associate Behavior Analysts (BCABA) or who are not yet certified, as well as train parents in ABA methods.

Although no credentialing system is perfect, the availability of the BCBA certification process has enabled many parents to hire staff for home programs who are highly skilled and very sophisticated in the use of ABA methods. This is a major advance from the "Buyer Beware" atmosphere which surrounded the field for many years and which is still a problem in areas where the rigorous Board Certification process has not become widely accepted or available. It is increasingly common for public school systems to hire staff members with this credential to supervise teachers and others who may not yet be certified.

Parents of preschool children with autism have more reason for optimism about the future of their child than ever before in the history of this disorder. There is much to celebrate. There is also great need for caution, however. Two major issues face every family seeking treatment for their child. First, in spite of the wider acceptance of the value of intensive professional training as a BCBA, there are not enough first-rate services to meet the needs of all of the children who need early intensive behavioral treatment. In some parts of the United States there are painfully few professionals who understand autism, and in many other parts of the world, resources are essentially nonexistent. As a result, many families are unable to locate adequate services for their child. Some families continue to fall prey to service providers who are neither honest nor competent. The lack of resources is a tragedy that can only be remedied by an ongoing program of education for professionals and parents alike and by public recognition that dollars spent on early treatment bring enduring economic as well as human benefits to society.

A second major issue facing families is the realization that even in the best of programs only about half of the children make enough progress to participate fully in the academic mainstream when they reach school age. The other children continue to need a great deal of educational support, although most do make more progress than they would have with less intensive treatment. This is a source of deep disappointment for many families, who understandably wish their preschool child to develop into one of those who does exceptionally well.

It is our belief that in the face of these possible obstacles to your child's educational progress, your best defense is to learn as much as possible about the effective uses of applied behavior analysis. Reading this book should give you the basic information you need to determine whether you want to seek out ABA treatment for your child, and to recognize a good program when you see one.

About This Book

The purpose of this book is to introduce you to the issues involved in the early, intensive behavioral treatment of children with autism and related disorders. The first chapter will introduce you to a few basics about behavioral treatment, early intervention, and the law. In Chapter 2 we will briefly summarize what the research tells us about the benefits of early intensive behavioral intervention. We will also give you a few basic principles about understanding research findings. Chapter 3 describes different models for early intensive behavioral intervention in autism, including home-based, center-based, and school-based models of treatment.

Chapter 4 looks at one of the complicated decisions parents have to make—whether their child's program should be home-based, center-based, or school-based. We will review some of the pros and cons involved in this decision making. Chapter 5 offers an overview of the curriculum that you might find in a good early intervention program. We have based this information on our own experience at the Douglass Developmental Disabilities Center. One of us (SLH) has been at the Center since 1972 and the other (MJW) since 1985. Because we know it well, we will often use examples from that setting to illustrate our points. For example, in Chapter 5 the curriculum description is based on our preschool program at the Douglass School. There are, of course, many other fine programs in the country, and we use the Douglass School only as an example.

Finally, Chapter 6 offers some guidelines for parents in deciding whether any program, whether home-based, center-based, or school-based, is suitable for their child. Although the chapters in this book are arranged in a sequential order, if you have a specific concern you can safely skip from one chapter to the next.

This book is intended for parents of children who have been diagnosed with one of the pervasive developmental disorders, or, as they are commonly called, autism spectrum disorders. Precise diagnosis of very young children is sometimes difficult, and for the purposes of this book it does not matter if your child is labeled as having autistic disorder, Asperger's disorder, childhood disintegrative disorder, or atypical autism (PDD not otherwise specified). Although the long-term prognosis for children in these four groups may be somewhat different, their early treatment is similar. If your daughter has Rett's disorder, her developmental course will be different than for children diagnosed with any of the other pervasive developmental disorders, and you will want to take that into account in her treatment. However, some of the information in this book will be useful to you as well.

Unless we are referring to a concern specific to one disorder, we will use the term "autism" or "autism spectrum disorders" to mean children on the broad spectrum of pervasive developmental disorders.

Sandra L. Harris and Mary Jane Weiss
Piscataway, New Jersey
January 2007

1 | An Introduction to Early Behavioral Intervention in Autism

The Yu Family

Harold and Grace Yu recall vividly the day their oldest child, Eddie, was born. It had taken more than a year for Grace to become pregnant and they were beginning to think it might not happen when Grace, to their delight, realized she was pregnant. After spending nine months happily preparing by painting the room, buying furniture, borrowing baby clothes from Harold's older sister, and buying a wonderful stuffed teddy bear, they were thrilled when the day arrived and Eddie became part of their lives. A perfect part, with tiny toes and fingers and a dear little face. Life seemed complete to Harold and Grace; their family was launched.

Eddie was a quiet, undemanding baby who cried when he was wet, hungry, or sick, but otherwise was a very easy baby. In fact, although they had planned to wait until Eddie was two years old before they tried to conceive again, once they realized how good he was they decided to try as soon as he turned one. By the time Eddie was fifteen months old, Grace was pregnant again.

A few months after she realized she was pregnant for the second time, Grace began to worry about Eddie. She was concerned that he had no words, rarely responded to his name, and unlike his cousin Anna, who was just four months older, he did not bring her things to show her. Her niece Anna often put favorite things into her mother's hand and looked up at her, smiling and naming the item. Although Eddie would bring Grace a broken toy or lead her by the hand to something he wanted and then push her hand toward the object, he didn't *seem very eager to show her things just to share them. He did delight in being tossed in the air and being tickled, but otherwise seemed happy to be left alone. Grace and Harold were perplexed by their son, but with the new baby on the way they were willing to let some time go by to see if his speech would improve and the social behaviors would follow. They assumed he was following his own clock.*

Just after Eddie's second birthday, his sister, Suzie, was born and Harold and Grace found themselves very busy with two small children to nurture. At times they would shake their heads in amazement at how different their children's temperaments were. Suzie demanded their attention, gazed in their eyes while she nursed, and cuddled close. Eddie, although he had been quiet and easy for so long, was now increasingly irritable. He had also developed a fascination with his hands and would turn them slowly in front of his eyes. On his birthday, he had been more upset than amused by the party and did not tear at the wrapping paper on his gifts or smear cake on his face the way other children had that day. Harold and Grace decided it was time to find out why their son was not yet speaking, often ignored them, and was doing unusual things with his hands. Their handsome boy showed no interest in toys and seemed to enjoy jiggling the bathroom doorknob most of all.

At Eddie's two-year checkup, the Yu family shared their concerns with the pediatrician. This visit was sobering for them. Rather than suggesting they wait a while to see how Eddie would do in time, their physician suggested that they take him to the child diagnostic center at their local children's hospital. She said that his behavior might be related to autism, but that they needed to see an expert to know for certain. After an agonizing six-week wait, they were able to see the developmental pediatrician and the child psychologist their physician had recommended. Over the course of several sessions, Eddie was given a complete evaluation and then the Yus met with the entire evaluation team, including the developmental pediatrician, clinical psychologist, social worker, and speech and language therapist.

Even though their pediatrician had raised the question of autism a couple of months earlier, it was still very painful for Harold and Grace to hear the diagnosis of autistic disorder. It was hard for them to listen to the rest of the conversation through the filter of their pain follow-

ing the diagnosis. The team members, who understood how difficult the meeting was for a family, gave them a written copy of the report so they could digest it later, as well as a written set of recommendations about what steps they needed to take next. They also scheduled a follow-up visit with the psychologist to help the family continue to make plans for Eddie.

Harold, who relied heavily on the computer at work, took it upon himself to find everything he could on the Internet about treating autism spectrum disorders in young children. As he commented to Grace, there was more information than he could digest and the challenge was to decide which websites were of high quality and which were not. He did find a site for the Autism Society of America (ASA) and that led him to a local chapter of the ASA where they could meet other parents in the same situation. Grace went to the bookstore and found several books for parents about how to educate their young child with autism. Their evenings were spent poring over this material and making plans to help Eddie. They were also spent with tears in their eyes, holding one another and promising they would somehow get through this trial.

When Harold and Grace returned to the psychologist's office a few weeks later, they understood far more about autism than they had before and were ready to talk with the psychologist about where to find early intensive treatment for Eddie using applied behavior analysis. The teaching method that impressed them the most, and had good research support, was applied behavior analysis (ABA), and this was the method they elected to use. The psychologist gave them a list of programs in their area that provided these services and commented that they were lucky to be living in a large metropolitan area where there were a variety of services available. People in more rural parts of the state often had to travel quite far to get help.

Is the Yu Family Like Yours?

The Yu family's experience in learning about their son's diagnosis and beginning the search for services for him is not unusual for parents of very young children on the autism spectrum. Thanks to a great deal of good research on diagnosis over several decades and considerable effort to educate professionals about autism spectrum disorders, it is increasingly likely that the family pediatrician will recognize when a child has a serious developmental problem such as autism. In addition, there is good research documenting the benefits of intensive early intervention for children with autism.

The Yu family obtained a state-of-the-art evaluation for Eddie. The psychologist administered the Autism Diagnostic Observation Schedule (ADOS) to Eddie (Lord, Rutter, DiLavore, & Risi, 1999). Grace and Harold sat on one side of the room and watched this session with concern as Eddie ignored the psychologist's efforts to engage him in simple games such as blowing bubbles that most children would enjoy. They were glad to see him imitate some of the things the examiner did such as rolling a car, and delighted when he giggled with pleasure during a simple tickling game, but were deeply concerned about the many colorful toys he ignored. The Yus were also interviewed with the Autism Diagnostic Interview (Lord, Rutter, & LeCouteur, 1994), a very detailed and lengthy questionnaire that, combined with the ADOS, made Eddie's diagnosis clear. For more information about these structured interviews for children and adults, see another book in the Woodbine House Topics in Autism Series, *Demystifying Autism Spectrum Disorders* (2004) by Dr. Carolyn Thorwarth Bruey.

The Yu family was exceptionally fortunate because they lived in a state that had good resources for children with autism. In many places in the United States and around the world they would not have found such excellent assessment and diagnostic services and might have been advised to seek treatment methods that would not have been so beneficial for Eddie. For example, they might have been told to try play therapy or a program placing an exclusive emphasis on sensory treatments. Neither of these approaches has documented *empirical* (research-based) support in the treatment of autism.

In spite of the helpful information that was available, the Yus were thrust into a complex and demanding situation almost over night. They had to deal with their intense emotional reactions when Eddie was given a serious diagnosis, and almost immediately had to start searching for the right educational program for him. There was no time to catch their breath! They had to live with mixed emotions. There was the pain of the diagnosis and the hope that the right program might be of major benefit to him. There was the anxiety of trying to identify a program for Eddie, and the relief that there was something specific they might do for him. The turmoil was intense and family life was turned topsy-turvy by those two words—autistic disorder.

What Is Early Intensive Behavioral Intervention?

Do not confuse early intensive behavioral intervention with the term "early intervention." Early intervention is a general term referring to services for infants and toddlers with all kinds of disabilities, while early intensive behavioral intervention is a very specific treatment shown to be helpful in treating autism. Currently, not all generic early intervention programs offer intensive behavioral intervention to young children with autism, although the number has increased in recent years. Some early intervention programs treat children with autism using other methods. Unfortunately, there is a dearth of good research to support these other interventions.

It may be helpful to dissect the phrase "early intensive behavioral intervention." "Early" always means beginning before the child turns five, usually before four, and preferably as young as possible. Children with autism are being identified at increasingly young ages and it is not uncommon for children aged two years or even eighteen months to be seen for treatment. "Intensive" describes the many, many hours of treatment that are required. The term "behavioral" refers to the use of applied behavior analysis, a special kind of teaching that will be described in the next section. Finally, the word "intervention" simply means treatment.

There are several features that make applied behavioral analysis (ABA) special in the treatment of young children with autism. One is the intensity of the treatment. It should be done for at least 25 to 40 hours a week with most of the teaching being done in a one-to-one teacher to child ratio. Second, ABA is a highly structured approach to teaching. Although much of the teaching is naturalistic in nature and capitalizes on a child's interests, it is not simply a "go with the flow" method. Rather, it is carefully designed and follows very predictable patterns of instruction. Third, there is minimal down time during which the child is not actively learning. Brief breaks are followed by brief lessons at a rapid pace. In addition, applied behavior analysis is based on well-studied principles of human learning and is designed to capitalize on the capacity of children to benefit from proven methods of instruction.

In the United States, the general term "early intervention" legally applies to services for infants and toddlers with disabilities from birth through the age of two years. Children with disabilities who are three and older are generally served by the special educational system rather than the early intervention system. However, in the autism field it is very common to hear the term "early intensive behavioral intervention" used to describe treatment services for any child up to school age. We will use the term early intensive behavioral intervention to refer to the treatment of any child with autism who is below kindergarten age.

What Happens During a Teaching Session?

As explained in the section above, the research-based procedures and methods known as applied behavior analysis are at the heart of intensive behavioral intervention for young children with autism. To help clarify what is meant by "applied behavior analysis," here is a brief overview of what goes on during a teaching session.

Initially, teaching sessions are done in a space that has been arranged for this purpose. It might be a corner of a child's room, a section of the classroom, or another reasonably quiet and distraction-free setting where the teacher can control the level of stimulation. Usually there will be a small table and chairs, although sometimes, especially with very young children and during naturalistic programs, a child may work on the floor or in a beanbag chair. The

structure should be determined by the child's needs.

The first step in working with any child is for the instructors to establish a relationship with that child. These instructors may include certified teachers, parents, and other family members, as well as concerned friends and members of the community who have been trained in ABA methods. In part, that means making yourself into the sort of fun person whom the child is likely to seek out and want to be with. We want our young students to light up when they see their instructors. With some children, that process of building a reinforcing relationship may happen quickly, but other children are much slower to warm up. In some cases it may mean the teacher or parent has to tolerate tantrums and tears until the child begins to accept our presence and then to delight in being with us. Once the working relationship is established, we can make increasingly greater demands on the child to attend to us and follow our instructions.

From early on, the education of a child with autism is usually a combination of 1) naturalistic methods that appear on the surface more like play than teaching, and 2) the very structured approach of *Discrete Trial Instruction* (DTI). DTI is used for teaching skills that may require repeated trials—for example, learning the names of objects. Naturalistic methods are best for encouraging spontaneous initiations and back and forth exchanges with another person. For example, we would teach a child to make spontaneous requests with naturalistic methods, but might teach the names of objects using discrete trials in which he can practice a skill multiple times.

Discrete Trial Instruction

DTI is one of many instructional techniques used in applied behavior analysis and is probably the best known teaching strategy. It is a critically important teaching method because it provides a very clear and simple framework for learning. With DTI's clear instructions and consequences, a variety of behaviors can be rehearsed. DTI is the most efficient and effective method of instruction for some early lessons that require memorization.

A teaching session using DTI involves a series of requests, tasks, or questions that are posed to the child. Each item to be taught is broken down into simple components in order to maximize the likelihood that the child will be able to respond. First the teacher gives an instruction such as "Do this" while she models a simple gesture such as clapping hands. Then, in the early trials, she reaches over, grasps the child's hands, and helps him clap. Gradually, she *fades* (phases out) this "prompt" until the child is responding independently to the command "Do this." She also gradually mixes hand clapping with other previously learned imitations such as foot stamping and head patting. After a correct response, the child is rewarded or "reinforced" for his good work. This reinforcement might include a tiny bit of a favored food, a few moments of play with a desired toy, or a sip of juice. It also includes words of praise such as "Great job," "Super work," or "Way to go." This praise is given with great enthusiasm.

Another important feature of DTI is mixing the old material the child has already mastered with new material. Initially the ratio is about 80 percent "old" material to 20 percent "new." This ratio gradually shifts with more new material in the mix to about a 50:50 mix. This process of mixing different old and new material is called "interspersal." The material that is intermixed may include additional previously learned examples of the same skill the child is mastering and other unrelated skills as well.

In addition, the teacher keeps a record of how many correct versus incorrect responses the child makes. Sometimes the teacher keeps "trial by trial" data, recording how the child does each time he is asked to perform the skill. More often, the teacher takes a "sample" of the child's performance, recording data for only some trials. The teacher uses these data to determine when to move on within the program. Because ABA does not rely on subjective opinions about progress, ABA is often referred to as a "data-based" technique.

Naturalistic Instruction

A number of different methods fall under the broad heading of naturalistic ABA teaching methods. These include:

1. Incidental Teaching,
2. the Natural Language Paradigm,
3. Pivotal Response Training, and
4. Natural Environment Training.

Incidental Teaching. *Incidental Teaching* was developed in the 1970s by Betty Hart and Todd Risley (1974). This is a data-based method for increasing the complexity of a child's language. The parent or teacher who uses this method first sets up an attractive environment. For example, there might be cool toys on a shelf that is out of the child's reach, but clearly visible. The adult waits for the child to show some interest in the toys either verbally or with gestures. She then prompts the child to elaborate on his initial response. If the child had pointed to the ball, the teacher might prompt him to say "ba" and then present the ball. For a more verbal child who said "ball," the prompt might expand the statement into "Want ball" or "blue ball." When the child responds to the prompt, the toy is provided and he is given an opportunity to play with the toy.

Incidental Teaching is easy to integrate into many daily routines. For example, you might start to play with a toy that your child likes and his request for it gives you the opportunity to work on language. Creating opportunities for incidental learning makes use of the child's natural environment, takes advantage of his motivation to respond, allows you to use naturally occurring reinforcers (rewards) such as holding the toy, and reinforces the child for initiating a behavior.

Natural Language Paradigm. Another naturalistic method, the *Natural Language Paradigm* (NLP) developed by Robert

Koegel and his colleagues (e.g., Koegel, O'Dell & Koegel, 1987), is effective for encouraging language in young children. In this empirically supported method, the child is presented with intrinsically interesting materials in a natural setting where we want to encourage him to play. Like Incidental Teaching, NLP emphasizes following the child's interests. During the course of playful interaction with toys that have captured the child's attention, the teacher or parent encourages him to use spoken language and elaborations of basic speech. The goals can vary over time from simply increasing vocalizations through modeling and reinforcement to teaching colors by providing items of different colors, or working on prepositions by describing the locations of items.

Pivotal Response Training. In *Pivotal Response Training* (Koegel & Koegel, 2005) a child is taught skills that are fundamental (or pivotal) to learning other new behaviors. Two of the primary skills targeted with this method are 1) increasing the child's motivation and 2) learning to use multiple cues.

Teaching a child to be a motivated learner will usually help him respond to the many different lessons he has to learn and master over time. Consequently, this approach devotes considerable effort to increasing a child's motivation to respond. Another important pivotal behavior is for the child to learn to respond to multiple cues. Children on the autism spectrum tend to be too narrowly attentive when looking at objects. They may focus only on a particular piece of jewelry their teacher wears as their way of remembering her or attend only to the color and not the size or shape of an object. If, for example, a child focuses in only on the color red rather than an object's other attributes, he will not do well at discriminating a red apple from a red toy fire engine. To address this problem, Pivotal Response Training teaches the child to recognize the many different dimensions of objects, including size, shape, texture, and so forth.

Another pivotal response is generalized imitation (that is, being able to imitate in any setting). Your child must learn not only to imitate on the command, "Do this," during a one-to-one session, but also to imitate on request in a group, and to imitate a broad range of behaviors including watching what other children are doing and copying them. For example, if the teacher gives an instruction that puzzles the child with autism, but he sees other children putting their materials in their desk and getting in line, that would cue him to do the same.

Natural Environment Training. Another treatment package with a naturalistic focus is Natural Environment Training (NET), which was developed by Mark Sundberg and James Partington (1998) as a way to teach verbal behavior to people with autism. NET is based on the work of psychologist B.F. Skinner and has important implications for teaching social skills as well as language. This approach has become best known for teaching language using a verbal classification system to organize the curriculum and places an initial emphasis on teaching a child to make spontaneous requests. The very user-friendly book by Drs. Sundberg and Partington explains the use of NET in detail. We have a couple of examples of using this approach to teach language in Chapter 5.

All of the naturalistic methods share the use of: 1) an attractive setting with toys and activities that are very appealing to the child, which builds the reinforcement into the interaction, **and** 2) interspersing (mixing) responses the child knows with new responses.

The Skills Taught Using Applied Behavior Analysis

The skills to be taught using applied behavior analysis include the full spectrum of activities essential to the child with autism. These range from self- help skills such as dressing and face washing to very complex social skills involved in play with other children. Speech, receptive language, and academic readiness skills such as matching, using a pencil, number concepts, and letter recognition can all be taught using these methods. Although these tasks may sound complex, they can usually be broken down into small units that are easier to teach than the whole skill at once. For example, teaching speech may begin with reinforcing any sounds the child makes, then gradually helping the child make those sounds more and more like a desired sound. The sounds can then be attached to objects as the child begins to label with simple words like "ball."

In addition to being used to teach new skills, applied behavior analysis can be used to help children with autism learn to control disruptive behaviors such as tantrums, stereotyped behavior such as body rocking or hand waving, and noncompliance. Chapter 5 describes a typical curriculum in more detail.

Who Needs Early Intensive Behavioral Intervention Services?

Every young child who is diagnosed with a pervasive developmental disorder (also called an autism spectrum disorder) including autistic disorder and pervasive developmental disorder not otherwise specified (sometimes called atypical autism) should receive early and intensive behavioral intervention services. Treatment should begin as soon as possible after the diagnosis is made. Although the specific components of treatment will vary depending on the child's needs, each of these children should be receiving ABA services. As discussed in the next chapter, the research documenting the benefits of these treatments is substantial, and the risks of failing to intervene before school age are very serious. One does not wait to see if a child will "outgrow" autism.

We cannot rely on a child's intelligence as measured by an IQ test to predict how he or she will respond to these teaching methods. It is certainly an advantage if your child is able to cooperate with this testing and shows signs of normal or near normal intelligence. However, we know many very young children who were initially classified as having mental retardation who responded well to teaching and are now functioning in the normal intellectual range. Furthermore, as Tristram Smith and his colleagues have shown (1997), even children with pervasive developmental disorders and severe mental retardation do better when they have intensive treatment than when they do not. Do not let your child's tested IQ score deter you from using applied behavior analysis.

Although we do not yet have research showing exactly what happens in the brain of a young child with autism who receives intensive teaching, we believe there are enduring changes for the better in how their brains function. It appears that with good teaching their brains are at least partially able to compensate for whatever the deficits were that gave rise to their autism. This potential for change, or "plasticity" as it is sometimes called, is one of the reasons we cannot assume that a child who tests in the mentally retarded range before treatment will remain in that category after treatment. We do not yet know which children will respond best to treatment and which will not. It is therefore essential that every young child have access to this opportunity.

As mentioned in the Introduction, intensive behavioral intervention can be helpful to children who have been diagnosed as having any of the disorders under the broad heading of pervasive developmental disorder (PDD) according to the criteria of the American Psychiatric Association in their *Diagnostic and Statistical Manual of Mental Disorders* (2000). This includes autistic disorder and atypical autism. It also includes Asperger's disorder. However, because children with Asperger's disorder are not as obviously impaired as children with other forms of PDD, they are sometimes not identified until school age. As a result, these children may not be recognized as needing services in the years before kindergarten. If you have a child with Asperger's disorder who is below kindergarten age, by all means seek early intensive behavioral intervention services for him.

What about Older Children?

Parents of older children with autism who have not received early intensive intervention often wonder whether it is too late to benefit their child. Applied behavior analysis is helpful for people with autism, regardless of their age. However, the most substantial changes in a child's developmental path are likely to occur during treatment at an early age. Perhaps because the brain loses some of its plasticity as children grow older, the gains for school-aged children and adolescents are more modest. In spite of this limit, it is important to know that behavioral treatment at any age can be highly beneficial. Every child deserves the best education possible.

The ways in which ABA methods are used typically differ based on a child's age. For example, unless they pose very unusual management problems, older children usually work in small groups and focus on different instructional content than younger children. The ABA methods are used to teach skills appropriate to the child's age. This can be seen in the choice of reinforcements (rewards) for good work. A very young child might work for a reward of chocolate pudding or tickles, and an older child might work for pennies to be used to buy a treat of his choice. Thus, the content and context may differ, but the teaching methods are based on the same scientific principles of human learning. See the book *Incentives for Change* by Lara Delmolino and Sandra L. Harris for information on creating motivational systems for people with autism.

How Is Intensive Behavioral Intervention Related to Early Intervention?

Today, generic early intervention services are considered essential for children with a wide variety of disabilities. Some children enter an early intervention program when they are tiny infants, particularly if they are known to have suffered traumas during the birth process or were born with disabilities such as Down syndrome that are evident from birth or very early in development. By contrast, children with autistic disorder, Rett's disorder, or pervasive developmental disorder not otherwise specified (atypical autism) may not be diagnosed until they are approaching their second birthday. In the case of Asperger's disorder or childhood disintegrative disorder, the diagnosis may be made later still. For a child like Eddie Yu, who has a diagnosis of autistic disorder, the early months may be uneventful and parents may be quite unaware that their child will need special services.

Once an infant or toddler is identified as possibly needing early intervention services, he is evaluated to determine whether he qualifies to receive early intervention services at public expense. Typically, a team of professionals with different areas of expertise will observe and test him to see whether he has significant developmental delays or is considered at risk of having delays. If the evaluation team finds significant delays, the infant or toddler is declared eligible for early intervention, and qualifies for a host of benefits and protections under the federal Individuals with Disabilities Education Act (IDEA), Part C.

Early intervention services may be provided in several different settings, including in the home, a school, a hospital, or a special clinic. One common way to describe early intervention programs is based on their location—in the home or outside of the home. Programs provided in the home are called "home-based," while those done in hospitals and other agencies may be called "center-based." Often early intervention programs combine these two approaches, with the center-based program providing direct service to the child and also teaching the parents what to do at home.

The specific services a child receives in an early intervention program will depend upon his needs. These services can include speech and language therapy, physical therapy, interventions to stimulate cognitive (intellectual) development, and so forth. Physicians, psychologists, educators, dietitians, physical therapists, occupational therapists, and social workers may all become involved in working with the child and family in an early intervention program.

Families who enroll their children in early intervention programs in the United States receive an Individualized Family Service Plan (IFSP). This is a document that families and professionals jointly develop. It specifies the short-term and long-term goals that parents and professionals would like to see the child achieve, as well as the treatment methods and therapies that will be used to help the child reach his goals, the assessment procedures that will be used to determine whether goals are met, and information about support to be provided to the family. This is similar to the Individualized Education Program (IEP) for school-aged children receiving special education, but is focused on the needs of very young children and their families.

Early intervention programs rely upon parents as active members of the child's treatment team. This is because it is considered essential that the child's learning be consistently supported throughout the day, and not just in treatment sessions. Parents are typically taught many of the treatment techniques being used by the professionals who serve the family. Parents may then carry out treatment sessions just as a professional might, or they can supplement the work of the professional, working to ensure a carry-over from the treatment session to the child's daily life.

For children with an autism spectrum disorder, early intervention program services typically focus on speech and language services, cognitive and social development, and behavior management. If there are problems with motor control or other specific deficits, suitable services would also be offered to meet those needs. However, very few early intervention programs offer intensive behavioral treatment. If you want those services for your child, you must shop for them. Again, early intervention is not the same as early intensive behavioral intervention! If a program does not meet your child's needs, you should look for resources that are appropriate. Don't settle for an inadequate program.

The next few sections explain how to find out what types of services your local early intervention program offers for children with autism, and offer suggestions as to what to do if the local program does not routinely offer intensive behavioral intervention for young children with autism.

What Does the Law Say?

The civil rights movement in the United States not only had a direct impact on the rights of people of color, women, and adults with disabilities, but also was part of a process that resulted in improved educational opportunities for children of all ages who have disabilities.

Your child's right to educational services varies with his or her age. The dividing line for services is the third birthday. Children younger than three years are typically served by the early intervention system, and those three years and older by the educational system. (Under the 2004 revisions to IDEA, there is now an option for some children to remain in early intervention until age five, but most transition out of it at age three.) It is important to know what the federal legislation says about the

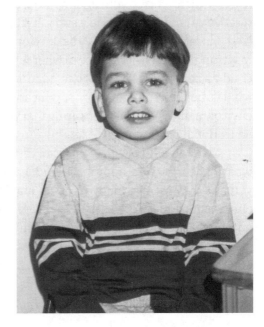

education of children at different ages so that you can ensure your child is getting the services to which he or she is entitled.

From birth though two years of age, your child's right to services is based on the Infants and Toddlers subsection (Part C) of the Individuals with Disabilities and Education Act (IDEA). That law gives federal assistance to states to support comprehensive and broadly based early intervention services. These services must meet a variety of criteria, including the use of a multidisciplinary team to conduct the assessment, and the creation of an individual treatment plan for each family (called an Individualized Family Service Plan or ISFP). All states provide treatment services for infants and toddlers. No matter where you live in the United States, you and your infant or toddler have the right to services. However, although some services such as evaluation and assessment are always free, states may charge families for direct intervention (e.g., therapies and specialized instruction) on a sliding fee scale.

After a child reaches the age of three years, his or her educational needs are covered by Part B, the portion of IDEA that concerns school-aged children. This legislation assures your child of the right to a free (at no cost to you) and "appropriate education" in the "least restrictive environment" necessary. It stipulates that an Individualized Education Program (IEP) be developed for your child, detailing in writing what services, done in what setting, will be provided your child as part of his "appropriate education." Since understanding what is meant by an "appropriate education" in the "least restrictive environment" is crucial to ensuring that your child benefits from his educational program, let's examine those terms in more detail.

The law allows a great deal of latitude for interpretation of what constitutes an appropriate education for every child, and you as a parent have many rights in making decisions about your child's education. For example, appropriate special education can go beyond academic instruction to include support needed to help your child master daily living skills and to enhance his social and emotional development. An extended school year longer than the 180 days typical in most school systems, home support, or residential treatment may all be deemed "appropriate" for some children.

Because the federal legislation does not dictate specific treatment for specific disorders, there is room for debate about what is "appropriate" for a child. You should know, however, that "appropriate" is usually not interpreted by early intervention and special education programs to mean "best." Instead, an "appropriate" education is usually interpreted as one that enables the child to receive some benefit from his educational program.

Similarly, there can be differences of opinion about what setting is "least restrictive." (The least restrictive environment, or LRE, is the educational setting that permits a child with disabilities to have the maximum contact with typically developing peers while making progress toward his educational goals.) Does the LRE mean included in a typical class in a public school at grade level? Placed in a special class in a public school? A private special education class? Home-based instruction? Any of these may be least restrictive for some children.

The only way to be certain you are acting in your child's best interests is to know the law in some detail. Your local school district must provide you with a written copy of all of your legal rights concerning your child's education. In addition, you can get a copy of your state's special education regulations from the state department of education. You are also entitled to have access to every report and other document that has been written about your child. As a parent, nothing should be kept secret from you. You must also give your consent prior to any evaluation of your child. If you do not agree to an evaluation, the school must go to a due process hearing in order to override your decision. In addition, you can request a due process hearing if you and the school disagree about other aspects of your child's program, including the least restrictive setting, the services provided, and whether or not assistive technology is provided for your child.

In sum, a series of federal laws have been enacted by the Congress of the United States which ensure that your child has the right to appropriate educational services from birth to age 21 years. For parents of young children with autism, however, most of the challenges lie not in finding some form of treatment for their child, but in finding *appropriate* treatment. Early intervention and preschool staff may not always have the needed expertise in treating autism spectrum disorders, professionals may disagree with parents about what constitutes appropriate treatment, or a community may lack programs that are proven to be effective.

Although IDEA has proved helpful to many families, it may not be sufficient to ensure that you will be able to obtain the services your child needs. Many families have had to resort to lawsuits, or the threat of such suits in order to obtain the program their child requires. On the other hand, some early intervention programs and school districts are remarkably helpful, and some have well-trained staff to serve families. Your own experience will hinge on where you live and the specific people with whom you deal. Expect to be served well, but be prepared to act assertively on your child's behalf if need be. Sometimes that action may include contacting a lawyer well versed in disability law.

Although ABA programs for young children with autism are often done at home, funding agencies can be reluctant to support a home-based rather than a center-based program. There are at least two major arguments to raise on behalf of home-based services. One is that many very young children are normally at home until they begin kindergarten. Related to this is the notion that many families prefer to have their young child at home and under close parental supervision until the child is of school age. Chapter 4 discusses in more detail the pros and cons of home-based and center-based treatment.

Working with Your School District or Early Intervention Agency

If you suspect or know that your child has a disorder on the autism spectrum and he is three or older, contact the office of your local school district and ask to speak to the person who can arrange an intake evaluation for your child. These professionals should work with you to evaluate your child's needs, develop an educational plan, identify potential placements, and help you make a placement decision. Not only do they have the legal obligation to serve your child after he turns three, they also are often caring people who want to do what is best for children. Many families receive a compassionate, highly intelligent, and helpful response from their local school district.

If your child is under three, your local early intervention program is responsible for your child's education. Although some of these agencies are responsive to the highly specialized needs of children with autism, many of them are not. That is, they may offer your child a general early intervention program, providing at most several hours of services a week, rather than the intensive behavioral intervention that most benefits young children with autism spectrum disorders. In our experience, the public schools have tended to be more alert to these special needs, although this is changing in some states. As a result, you may need to assume much more initiative (and expense) for your child prior to the age of three years. If you are very fortunate, you may live in a school district that recognizes that money spent on the intensive treatment of a two-year-old will often save thousands of dollars later. Recognizing this cost-efficient (not to mention humane!) intervention, they may serve your child even before he turns three. See our discussion in Chapter 4 of how to enlist the help of a reluctant school district.

Be open to professional input. Try to find professionals you trust and then work with them collaboratively, but always keep your highest priority in mind—your child's welfare. Remember that no one can be as loving and devoted an advocate for your child as you can.

What about Other Treatments?

This book is designed to help parents understand the importance of using applied behavior analysis in treating young children with autism, and to help them set up or find an appropriate program for their child that uses ABA. However, many different approaches have been tried in the treatment of autism, and your school district or early intervention program may very well use something other than ABA in working with young children with autism. What should you do if you encounter this situation?

It is important to find out whether any program proposed for your child is based on research proving that it is effective. Every quality program should also be able to explain in detail their teaching methods and conceptual framework. In Chapter 6, we discuss how to evaluate a potential placement for your child. Although our criteria in that chapter focus on ABA programs, they will also be useful in evaluating other approaches.

Parents Speak

When I first heard the word "autistic," my son was 18 months old and running around the pediatrician's office. At first I thought the doctor was totally out of her mind. Who knew anything about autism? I certainly didn't. Yes, he was doing odd things and yes, he was developmentally delayed, but autistic—no! All kinds of thoughts were running through my mind on the drive home from her office. Through my tears, I wondered how the most beautiful baby boy I had ever seen could possibly have this horrible disorder. I felt I was handed a life sentence. I wondered if he would ever play baseball, have friends, talk, and call me Mommy. I wondered if I would ever dance with him at his wedding. Finally, I began to read and read and I haven't stopped yet.

☙❧

I still remember that drive home from the neurologist's office as though it were yesterday. Bang! Your kid has autism. Here is a list of schools where you can take him. Maybe he said more, but I didn't hear it. All I heard was "Your kid has autism," and I thought it meant he had no future. I must have cried for a week.

☙❧

My wife and I knew before the doctor even said anything that Tom probably had autism. I had been to the library and done a lot of reading. We figured it out before the doctors said anything. So, when the news came we were ready.

◌

I still can't get over it. How could this child, smaller than a minute, have so much wrong with her brain? I wasn't going to let that happen. We started right away with treatment. She was only thirty months old and so we had people come to the house to work there. The first few weeks she hollered for hours. But, after that she settled down and seemed much calmer. It got so she would hug the therapist and then run and get the little chair.

◌

In retrospect I think that every doctor who saw our son knew what they were looking at, but they referred us on to the next doctor on the checklist without telling us. It would have saved us a lot of time if they had told us their suspicions.

My wife and I were ushered into a doctor's office and the door was closed. The doctor handed each of us a copy of a thick, computer-generated document, sat behind the desk, and began reading from her copy of the diagnosis—word for word, typos and all—without looking up at us.

I felt a deep sorrow for the first two years or so. When I was happy I wasn't as happy as I used to be; when I was sad I was a lot sadder than I used to be. It was the first thing I felt when I woke up in the morning and the last thing I felt at night when I went to sleep.

◌

At his eighteen-month check-up, my son was seen by my pediatrician's practitioner, who reassured me he was just a late talker. I began asking all the young mothers in my neighborhood about their children, and they too said boys talk later than girls. Thinking that my son's lack of language and increasing odd behaviors were just his personality, I felt fairly confident there was nothing wrong. Meanwhile, his eye contact diminished, his love of rocking and swinging became obsessive, he often acted as if he were deaf, and he would occasionally laugh hysterically at nothing apparent. At his second birthday, all the guests played in our backyard while my son wandered off examining the vinyl siding on our house.

The pediatric neurologist's explanation of my son's diagnosis was both shocking and perplexing. I was so convinced my son was merely language delayed that the word "autism" hit me like a cold shower.

෧෨

We took our son to a major child development center for a comprehensive evaluation. When they said the "A" word it was like being told it was incurable cancer. It was terrifying, confusing, and heartbreaking. Our search for answers began the next day with my husband's visit to the local library.

The things that helped us the most in beginning the work with our son were:

1. Getting a clear, direct, and blunt diagnosis of Autism Spectrum Disorder.
2. Finding Catherine Maurice's book **Let Me Hear Your Voice.**
3. Beginning a program of applied behavior analysis and speech therapy quickly.

References

American Psychiatric Association. (2000). *Diagnostic and statistical manual of mental disorders (4th ed., Training)*. Washington, DC: Author.

If you want to read the criteria professionals use to diagnose Pervasive Developmental Disorders, go to the library and look at this book.

Bruey, C. T. (2004). *Demystifying autism spectrum Disorders: A guide to diagnosis for parents and professionals.* Bethesda, MD: Woodbine House.
>   In laymen's language, this book clearly explains what is involved in reaching a diagnosis of one of the five autism spectrum disorders.

Delmolino, L. & Harris, S. L. (2004). *Incentives for change: Motivating people with autism spectrum disorders to learn and gain independence.* Bethesda, MD: Woodbine House.
>   This book describes a variety of motivational systems for children and adults on the autism spectrum.

Maurice, C., Green, G., & Luce, S.C. (eds.) (1996). *Behavioral intervention for young children with autism: A manual for parents and professionals.* Austin, TX: Pro-Ed.
>   A good book on treatment for young children with autism. It includes a chapter by Mark Williamson on legal issues in funding programs. If you run into problems getting the services you want for your child, take a look at his chapter. In general, it is a fine and useful book.

Smith, T., Eikeseth, S., Klevstrand, M., & Lovaas, O.I. (1997). Intensive behavioral treatment for preschoolers with severe mental retardation and pervasive developmental disorder. *American Journal on Mental Retardation, 102,* 238-249.
>   This is the article we mentioned on the benefits of applied behavior analysis for children who have pervasive developmental disorders and severe mental retardation.

Sundberg, M. L. & Partington, J.W. (1998). *Teaching language to children with autism or other developmental disabilities.* Pleasant Hill, CA: Behavior Analysts, Inc.
>   See this book for information about Natural Environment Training

Other Articles Cited in the Chapter

Hart, B. & Risley T. R. (1974). Using preschool materials to modify the language of disadvantaged children. *Journal of Applied Behavior Analysis, 7,* 243-256.

Koegel, R. L., O'Dell, M. C., & Koegel, L.K. (1987). A natural language teaching paradigm for nonverbal autistic children. *Journal of Autism and Developmental Disorders, 17,* 187-200.

Koegel, R.L. & Koegel, L.K. (2005). *Pivotal response treatments for autism.* Baltimore, MD: Brookes Publishing Co.

Lord, C., Rutter, M., & LeCouteur, A. (1994). Autism Diagnostic Interview-Revised: A revised version of a diagnostic interview for caregivers of individuals with possible developmental disorders. *Journal of Autism and Developmental Disorders, 24,* 659-685.

Lord, C., Rutter, M., DiLavore, P. C., & Risi, S. (1999). *Autism diagnostic observation schedule - WPS edition (ADOS-WPS).* Los Angeles: Western Psychological Service.

2 | Does Early Intensive Behavioral Intervention Work?

Searching the Internet

Angelica Ruiz, a high school English teacher, had a BA degree in English literature and a master's degree in secondary education. Although she often e-mailed her friends and sometimes shopped online, she had not considered the Internet a place where she wanted to spend much time. Now, with a three-year-old daughter, Fernanda, who had just been diagnosed as having pervasive developmental disorder not otherwise specified (PDD-NOS) she found herself wading through a maze of websites, chat rooms, and home pages, searching for information about how to help her daughter. With her husband, Fernando, an Army captain away on an overseas assignment, much of the task of caring for Fernanda fell to Angelica. She found herself pushed to learn new skills and make many decisions by herself. Her husband often called and they e-mailed daily, but it was Angelica who had taken Fernanda for her diagnosis and extensive evaluations and who now had to take the lead in finding the right treatment for her daughter.

When she entered "autism" in her search engine, she got back more "hits" than she knew what to do with. As she began to sift through the websites, she found a great deal of advice, some of it contradictory, from one site to the next. There were many sites that were essentially one person's opinion and Angelica wondered why she should give so much weight to the writings of someone she had never met and who might or might not know much about autism. Although other people's experiences were interesting, she wanted to know what the research showed as helpful, so that is where she focused her search.

The local bookstore had a couple of books that Angelica found useful. One by Catherine Maurice described her personal encounter with autism, the various therapies she had been offered, and the applied behavior analysis approach (ABA) which ended up being the most helpful to her children. After she read this book, Angelica did a more careful search for other sources on ABA. This information ultimately led her to decide on ABA as the treatment she wanted for Fernanda.

Angelica's search for the term "applied behavior analysis" led her to some interesting chat room discussions. It also helped her find the name of Ivar Lovaas, a now-retired professor of psychology at UCLA who did groundbreaking research on the treatment of very young children with autism. His research showed that early intensive use of ABA made a major impact on the development of about half of the children who were part of his study. That finding was encouraging to Angelica and she reported it to Fernando that night when they spoke. He agreed that ABA sounded like the way to go for their little girl.

As she continued her research on ABA, Angelica found that while Dr. Lovaas was the pioneer in the field, a number of other studies had been done since then that also showed clear benefits for children who received ABA treatment while they were very young. With their goals now clear, Angelica, with Fernando's love and emotional support, set out to find an ABA program in their area that would accept Fernanda.

What Does the Ruiz Family Search Mean for You?

It is not unusual for parents of young children with autism to learn a great deal about treatment options on the Internet. However, the problem with information from the Internet is that there is no quality control. Anyone can write anything. It is impossible to know which programs that are described on the Internet are good and which are not. You cannot tell who is honest and who wants to make a buck or attract attention to him- or herself. The reader has only the individual opinions of strangers whose children may or may not resemble her own.

Although the Internet serves a valuable function in sharing information, it is less helpful in ensuring that this information has been carefully evaluated. The buyer must beware! Recognizing this limitation of the Internet, Angelica went to the library to look up information in professional journals. At a large bookstore that had a section of books on special education, she found several paperback books that were very helpful and that were written with parents in mind. That reading was helpful to her in reaching a decision about Fernanda's treatment. However, not everyone is prepared to plow through professional journals or buy books. Rather than turning to the library or a bookstore, some parents prefer to ask the opinion of a trusted professional. Regardless of how you get the facts about your child's options, it is important to ensure that you know what you are doing when you select your child's program.

It is probably also a good idea to check things out in more than one source. For example, if you read something on the Internet, look it up in a book as well. If one professional makes a suggestion about a treatment, ask another for his or her opinion too. Your local autism society, the national Autism Society of America, and brochures provided by various treatment programs may also be helpful. After a while, you will learn whom you can trust, but until that happens, keep a skeptical attitude.

In this chapter, we briefly describe the research on the behavioral treatment of young children with autism. We will also suggest some questions you can ask when you evaluate the claims that people make about any treatment method. You don't need a doctorate to do your own research! This chapter is intended to help you be a well-informed consumer of professional services.

What Happens to Children Who Receive Early Intensive Behavioral Intervention Services?

The very good news is that many children who receive intensive behavioral services at an early age do very well in that treatment. Some children make substantial gains in intelligence, social

skills, and adaptive behavior. However, there are also many other children whose gains are more modest. Even as we celebrate the improvement in our ability to treat autism, it is important to recognize that some children make limited gains, and they continue to need highly specialized services throughout their lives. While you work toward maximum benefit for your child, you must remember that the degree of change is very individual. Some children will make rapid progress, and other children will make slow and modest gains. We often cannot tell before treatment starts which children will make quick gains and which will progress more slowly. Still, it is important to put maximum effort into the treatment of every child. We need to know that we have done the best that we can for each child regardless of her long-term outcome.

Because of the very human tendency to celebrate our success, it is often easier for professionals to remember and focus more on their best outcomes when talking about their programs, and to put less emphasis on the children who make slower, more limited progress. People also want to make families feel better and sometimes they do that by playing down the sad fact that not every child achieves the best possible, hoped-for outcome through applied behavior analysis. Again, be skeptical and careful. Don't let one professional's charisma outweigh the need to collect as much information as you can.

As a parent, your most important objective will be the gains *your* child makes—not the best a school has produced, or the average for children in a given classroom, or children with autism in general. It is the outcome for your son or your daughter that matters most deeply and personally. In order to be realistic about your child's outlook, you need to know the facts about the full range of possible outcomes from a treatment program. Then, you can work toward the best, but understand that there are no guarantees for your child, or any child. No one knows when a child walks through the door how she is going to respond to treatment. If someone promises you huge gains, run fast in the other direction.

The Lovaas Study

What has research found about children with autism who have participated in intensive applied behavior analysis treatment from early childhood? To answer that question, we turn first to the most important study in the field, the research Professor Ivar Lovaas did at UCLA. In 1987, Lovaas published a paper in a professional journal that was to have far reaching influence on the field of autism. In this paper he reported on his work with 38 young children with autism. One of the requirements for being included in the study was that at the beginning of treatment the children had to be younger than 40 months of age if they were mute (not speaking) or younger than 46 months old if they had echolalia (parroting back speech). The children were divided into two groups. One group of 19 children, called the "Intensive-Experimental Group," received at least 40 hours a week of one-to-one treatment for at least two years. The other group of children, called the "Minimal-Treatment Control Group," had not more than 10 hours a week of one-to-one instruction during the two-year period.

Before the children started treatment and again when they were between 6 and 7 years old, their abilities in different areas such as intelligence and adaptive skills were measured a number of times. The treatment procedures used by the therapists in Lovaas's study were based on the principles of applied behavior analysis. In the earliest phase, the instructors attempted to reduce the children's disruptive behavior such as their tantrums, to increase their compliance with instructions, to teach them to imitate what other people did, and to teach them simple toy play. In addition, family members were taught the behavioral methods being applied by the staff so that they could be part of the treatment team. The second-year curriculum focused on expressive and abstract language and learning how to play with other children. In their third year of instruction, children were taught to express emotions, worked on pre-academic readiness skills, and learned how to acquire new skills by watching other children engage in a behavior (sometimes called observational learning). When they were ready, children were moved into regular preschool classes, and then into regular educational classes whenever possible.

What Professor Lovaas learned from this study continues to influence the education of young children with autism two decades later. He found that nearly half (47 percent) of the children in the intensive treatment condition were functioning at a normal level intellectually, and were in regular education classes when they were reevaluated at 6 to 7 years of age. Only one child in the minimal treatment group made the gains in intelligence and educational achievement found in the intensive treatment group. The results of Lovaas's study suggest that 10 hours or less of intensive teaching is not enough to make the difference for children with autism, but 40 hours or more of this instruction can lead to major changes for some children. It does not tell us what 30 hours or what 20 hours a week might do, only about the difference between 10 and 40 hours.

In addition to studying the children during their early childhood, Dr. Lovaas and his colleagues kept in touch with them over the years. In 1993, Lovaas and his colleagues John McEachin and Tristram Smith described their long-term follow-up of the children who had participated in the Intensive Experimental Group. At an average age of 13 years, the intensive treatment children who had made early gains continued to hold their own. In fact, 8 of the 19 children were now described as "indistinguishable" from other children their age on measures of intelligence and adaptive skills. It is very heartening to know that the progress they made in the preschool years was not lost by the time these youngsters were entering adolescence. It is also important to note that none of the children who had been in the control group had achieved this level of functioning.

In sum, Lovaas's research shows that intensive behavioral intervention at an early age enabled nearly half of his young participants to achieve essentially normal intellectual and academic functioning. The much poorer performance of the comparison group supports the argument that these changes were not simply the result of getting older, going to school, and so forth. The highly specialized treatment was necessary to bring about major change.

Other Studies on Early Intensive Behavioral Treatment

Although Dr. Lovaas's study is one of the most scientifically rigorous reports of the benefits of early intensive behavioral intervention for children with autism, it is not the only study to find clear benefits from applied behavior analysis. For example, there is a report from the Princeton Child Development Institute in New Jersey, a program for children with autism directed by psychologists Patricia Krantz and Lynn McClannahan. See Chapter 3 for a brief description of their program. Krantz, McClannahan, and their colleagues, Edward Fenske and Stanley Zalenski, followed the progress of 9 children who began intensive behavioral intervention before 60 months of age, and 9 who started treatment after 60 months of age. Their results showed that the children who started treatment before they were 5 years old had a better outcome than those who started later. This study highlights the importance of beginning treatment at an early age. Waiting until a child with autism is ready to enter kindergarten is much too late to begin treatment. Although older children benefit from treatment, they do not typically show the benefits of children who start when they are very young.

A 2005 study by psychologists Glen Sallows and Tamlynn Graupner provided considerable support for Dr. Lovaas's earlier findings. In a study of 24 young children with autism in Wisconsin and using the same basic approach as Dr. Lovaas, including many hours of weekly treatment, they found that 48 percent of the children were in a regular classroom by age 7 years.

In another outcome study, Dr. Tristram Smith and his colleagues examined the impact of intensive treatment versus parent training in ABA on young children with autistic disorder or PDD-NOS. Although the two groups were similar when the study began, after treatment the children who received intensive ABA were superior to the children in the other group on measures including intelligence, visual-spatial skills, language, and academic skills. These researchers did not show gains as great as those in the Lovaas study, perhaps because they provided fewer hours of treatment and perhaps because the children as a group had lower IQ scores before treatment.

At our own program in New Jersey, the Douglass Developmental Disabilities Center, we followed 27 children for 4 to 7 years after they left our preschool program. We found that those who had higher IQ scores at admission or who were younger when they started were more likely to be in a regular education class at follow up than were those who had lower IQs or were older at intake. These were not, however, perfect correlations and some older children did better than some younger ones and some children whose initial IQs were quite low did better than others with higher IQs. Thus, although a child's age and IQ are predictive of outcome, they are imperfect predictors. There is a brief description of our program in Chapter 3.

Jane Howard and her coauthors reported on a 2005 study which compared intensive ABA treatment with intensive eclectic treatment and with a third group of children who were enrolled in public school special education classes. (Eclectic treatment in this context refers to using a variety of different teaching methods with no single central organizing principle and often little, if any, research support.) Although the groups were similar at the beginning of the study, after treatment the children who received intensive ABA had higher scores than the other two groups on tests of intelligence, language, and adaptive behavior such as play, self-help, and social skills. The eclectic group and the special education class group did not differ from each other. This study provided additional support for the benefits of ABA when compared to a generic special education model or to an intensive, but non-ABA model.

Taken as a group, these studies all provide encouraging support for the potential value of using intensive behavioral treatment for young children with autism.

Thinking about Research

This chapter is intended to give you the skills to be your own judge of scientific research. As the parent of a child with

autism, it is vitally important that you know how to evaluate the claims on which your child's treatment is based. There are many unsubstantiated claims in the field of autism. You need to know who stands on solid ground when she makes claims about a treatment and who does not. Not everyone who gives you bad advice wishes to de-

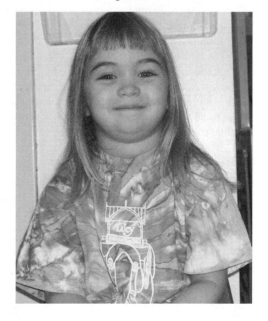

ceive you; they may simply be ignorant about the best treatments for autism. There are, however, some people who probably care more about taking your money than helping your child. Regardless of their motivation, some people are not operating in your child's best interests, and the task of protecting her falls to you. Be a questioning, critical consumer.

Table 2-1 summarizes some of the vocabulary you can use to think about research and Table 2-2 on page 38 provides a list of questions to ask about research studies.

Table 2-1 | A Primer of Common Research Terms

Adaptive Skills: Skills such as self-help, play, and social behaviors that help the child adapt to the demands of the environment.

Comparison Group: This term is sometimes used to describe a treatment condition that is used as a contrast with the "experimental" treatment under study. For example, if it has been shown that one treatment works well, that proven treatment might be used as a comparison for a new treatment that is being developed. Children in the comparison group would get the proven treatment and children in the experimental group the new treatment.

Control Group: In a research design, the control group is sometimes given no treatment or sometimes given a different treatment than the "experimental" group. A control group is used to show that common factors such as the passage of time, being in a classroom, or receiving adult attention are not the reason for the change in the child's behavior. Sometimes the term control group is used to describe a "comparison" group (see above).

Experimental Group: The experimental group is exposed to the treatment procedure under study. Their performance is contrasted with people in a comparison group (see above) or control group (see above) to learn if there is any advantage to being in the experimental condition.

Experimenter: The experimenter is the person who conducts a study. For example, Professor Ivar Lovaas is the experimenter who did an important study on the use of applied behavior analysis for treating children with autism.

What Does the Study Show?

The first question to ask about an intervention that is suggested for your child is whether there is any research showing that it does, in fact, do what its supporters claim and whether that research was any good. In good research, there is a comparison between two different experiences in order to find out whether the new treatment works. Some research compares what happens when one group of children receives the treatment (the experimental group) and a sec-

IQ: The term "IQ" is an abbreviation of the words "Intelligence Quotient." An IQ is a measure of a person's intelligence on a test that has been designed specifically for measuring IQ. For children with autism, these tests are usually given individually by a highly skilled school or clinical psychologist trained in this kind of testing. It is important that the examiner be experienced in testing children on the autism spectrum, as these children may need a great deal of patient support if they are to respond at their best. An experienced examiner will also know which test is most appropriate for a specific child.

Participant: A participant is a person who takes part in a research study. Some people use the term "subject" to mean the same thing. Participants may be in either the experimental or control groups (see above). In a good study, participants do not usually choose which condition they will join. Instead, they are assigned randomly.

Replication: Replication means repetition. A replication of a research study is a repeat of that study. Often replications are done in new places by people other than the original researcher. That is called an independent replication and when it finds pretty much the same thing as the original study, we feel more confidence in the original finding.

Treatment: A treatment is what the experimenter does to the participant (see above) to try to bring about change. For example, a treatment might be the use of applied behavior analysis for six months or the use of a drug.

ond group has no treatment at all (control group). However, these days it is often difficult to find parents who are willing to withhold all treatment from their child and just hang around waiting for a few years to see what happens! In addition, we know that children rarely if ever "outgrow" autism, and early studies have shown that children who receive minimal treatment make few gains.

As a result, it is common for studies on the treatment of autism to compare two different treatments rather than comparing one treatment to an untreated control group. For example, there might

---

Table 2-2 | Some Questions to Ask about Research

1. What claims are being made about this treatment?
(e.g., the treatment improves speech, decreases behavior problems, prepares children to enter kindergarten)

2. Is there research to support the claims being made?

3. Who took part in the research?
(e.g., diagnosis, age, gender, IQ, speech of the children)

4. How did the experimenters measure change in the children? (e.g., educational placement, IQ, speech development, adaptive skills)

5. Were measures of skills made both before and after treatment? (If only made after, it is impossible to know how the child would have done before treatment)

6. What did they do to the children during the study?
(Is there enough detail to tell what happened?)

7. Who did the treatment? (e.g., teacher, psychologist, undergraduate assistant, speech and language specialist, special education teacher, physician?)

8. Has there been a replication?
(Have other scientists repeated the finding?)

9. Does this study apply to my child?

be an experimental treatment group and another group which participates in the standard special education curriculum offered in the community. Or, as in the study by Dr. Smith and his colleagues described above, one group of children received intensive ABA and the other group was provided with parent training in ABA.

Is There Enough Information?

As you evaluate the information being offered to you about a treatment, ask yourself how much detail is provided about the treatment procedures used in the study. That detail will help you decide whether the treatment matches your own child's needs. Was the treatment done one-to-one with one adult and one child or was it done in a group? If it was done in a group, is your child ready to work in a group, or does she need one-to-one help? Were there typically developing peers in the class or only children with autism? What skills did the teacher in the study have? Does the treatment program where you want to enroll your child have staff with training comparable to that of the people who did the work in the study? How well does the kind of information taught to children in the study match the needs of your child?

How Did They Decide the Children Changed?

Another question to ask is how the investigators measured change in the children. There are many possible ways to evaluate a child's progress. These include: changes in intelligence as measured by IQ tests; changes in adaptive skills such as being able to get dressed independently or to buy an item at the store; changes in academic skills such as reading, math, and writing; improved use of expressive and receptive language; and so forth. Objective tests such as those that measure IQ tend to be more *reliable,* with different examiners reporting very similar scores when the testing is done fairly close in time. More subjective measures such as teacher or parent ratings of quality of play or relationships with peers are somewhat more vulnerable to bias or expectation effects. (For example, if a teacher expects the child to improve because she has started a new treatment, that could affect the teacher's observations of what is actually happening). When carefully done, however, these ratings based on judgments can yield more nuanced information about the quality of behavior than do the more structured tests. When studies report changes based on subjective measures, it is important to find out how reliable the ratings were when two or more raters reported on the same child.

The child's educational placement might also be used to measure change. Did the children enter a regular classroom? A special education class? One problem with using class placement as a measure of outcome is that school systems differ in their expectations for when a child is ready to be fully included. Some schools will integrate every child in a regular class regardless of the degree of disability, while others are reluctant to do so. That can vary even within a state. We find some schools in New Jersey are very ready to take children in their inclusive classes when they graduate from our preschool, but other school districts want to put comparable children in a special class. In addition, a child may be in an inclusive class with varying levels of support. At one end of the continuum, this support can involve a full-time classroom assistant whose full effort is devoted to the child with autism. Under somewhat less supported conditions, there may be a "shadow" who oversees the child's performance but only intervenes when essential, and who may work with a group that includes the child with autism and her peers as well. Finally, a child may be placed in a typical classroom with no special assistant assigned for support. So, class placement by itself is not a sufficient measure of outcome.

How Do These Children Compare to Mine?

You should find out about the particular children who were in the study. How do they compare to your child? Consider such factors as the average age, IQ, diagnosis, and whether or not the children had any language. We know there is a lot of variation in children

who are given a diagnosis of one of the autism spectrum disorders. Even within a category such as autistic disorder or Asperger's disorder, there is variation.

Differences in outcome reported by studies may sometimes be the result of those differences. If the children we include in our research sample are older or perform differently on a test of intelligence than those in another person's study, that difference could account for differences in our ultimate results. If children with better skills before treatment do better after treatment, it may not mean that the treatment was more effective, but only that people who start with higher skills end up with higher skills. Be very careful to explore who the children were who were part of the study. Remember that the rich get richer and bright children with autism are likely to make greater gains than those who are less bright.

Can the Findings Be Replicated?

You will hear the word replication used sometimes in research jargon. It simply means repeated. It is important that researchers in other places be able to replicate, or repeat, the findings that come from one scientist. When a study is replicated, the scientific community has even greater confidence in it than when one person has done the research in only one setting. For example, the fact that other people, in independent research settings, have reported findings that support the work of Dr. Lovaas increases our confidence in applied behavior analysis.

What about Treatments That Cannot Be Studied?

Be wary of people who claim that their treatment technique for children with autism cannot be studied. Sometimes that claim is used as a way to evade the responsibility of doing research. In other cases, people may make this claim because they recognize that their methods may not stand up under careful scrutiny. If a procedure is useful, there should be a way to measure the benefits.

Taking Part in Research

There is a lot of research going on to improve our educational methods for children with autism and to better understand what causes the various kinds of pervasive developmental disorders. If you and your child are asked to participate in one of these studies, look carefully at the credentials of the person who invites you into the study. Does this person have the necessary scientific background to conduct the research? If the person is a graduate student doing research under supervision, does the professor have the skills to ensure the work goes well? How will the investigator evaluate your child's progress and decide whether your child is benefiting? If the study is going to take a significant amount of your child's time, it is especially important that you have enough details to be certain it is a good study that has a fair chance of helping your child.

When in doubt about a study, ask questions. Also, remember that you can say "no" to any study that you do not believe is in your child's best interests. Be very skeptical of someone who tries to pressure you into participation or who promises you benefits that seem unrealistic. You should be given a written description of the study and be asked to give your written consent to participating. If you are not offered that information, you probably do not want to be part of the project.

All of these cautions aside, it is through good research that we have made so much progress in the treatment of children with autism. Dr. Lovaas's work hinged on the generosity of 38 families who allowed their children to be part of his project. What Ivar Lovaas and those families did stands to be of personal benefit to you and your child. If you can help a good scientist do good work, we hope you will do so. The best place to look for these opportunities is at a university or medical school in your area.

Summing Up

A number of scientists in different parts of the world have shown that early intensive behavioral intervention can be of substantial benefit to many children with autism. The research suggests that this intervention should begin at an early age and be very intensive in nature. If someone offers you a nonbehavioral treatment, they should be able to show you data from a well-designed study indicating that their method performs at least as well as intensive behavioral treatment. If you use that as your measuring stick, you will be able to make good judgments about what is in your child's best interests.

Parents Speak

My son needed help and he needed it now. In almost all my readings, early and intensive therapy was very important. I read about Lovaas and his research with children using applied behavior analysis and the good results he was getting. After reading many articles and books, ABA kept coming up. I decided this was the way to go and I wanted to try it. I want my son to reach his full potential and I am going to do everything in my power to see that he does. Through friends I met in the early intervention program I went to, I found out about the home-based services offered at a nearby center. I got in touch with them and began a home-based program. My son was 27 months and we started with 2 hours a week and increased to 28 hours by the time he started school at age 3.

༄

I'm a history professor and I do a lot of reading. So when we found out Rob needed therapy, I read a lot and asked a lot of questions before we started him on applied behavior analysis. I needed to be certain this was the right thing to do. There were lots of people making a lot of claims. One of the things I liked when I talked to the director at the program where Rob goes is that she didn't make any promises. She said they would work very hard with him and with us, but that she could not make any promises. I liked the fact that she was honest with us. The fact is, he has made pretty good progress, but it hasn't been magic. He still has a long way to go.

༄

You might say my son is one of the miracle children. He has made fabulous progress in the last two years. This fall he is going to a regular kindergarten full time. I thank the Lord and a wonderful group of teachers for that. But I see other children who started when he did who have not done so well. It breaks my heart for their parents. I know it must hurt them when they see how well Rob has done and their child has not. I try not to talk about him too much with them.

༄

I just didn't know what to do after we found out about Allison. We were lucky to have a good doctor who knew what to tell us. She sent us to the school district and they were wonderful. They found a program for Allison and she has made good progress. I'm not much of a reader, but the way they explain things to us, I don't have to be.

We observed several schools in operation before deciding which was the right one for our son. Applied behavioral analysis, especially in its earliest phase, can be hard for a parent to watch. It has it origins in behavior modification, and it isn't the way parents want to teach their child. But we understood that if "normal" methods could have worked with our son we wouldn't be looking for a special school. Our son was enrolled at the age of 2 years, 10 months at a private placement at our own expense. The school district continued his placement and picked up his expenses when he turned three.

You should choose a program that is data-based. Any claims of success are only useful if controlled experiments are done on a relatively large sample of children. One child benefiting from a particular remedy is not a reason to pursue it. Many hundreds of children benefiting, however, as is the case with ABA, is certainly worth pursuing.

References

If you want more information on the studies mentioned in this chapter, here are the references to the original studies on which our descriptions are based.

Fenske, E.C., Zalenski, S., Krantz, P.J., & McClannahan, L.E. (1985). Age at intervention and treatment outcome for autistic children in a comprehensive intervention program. *Analysis and Intervention in Developmental Disabilities, 5,* 49-58.

Harris, S.L. & Handleman, J. S. (2000). Age and IQ at intake as predictors of placement for young children with autism: A four to six year follow-up. *Journal of Autism and Developmental Disorders 30,* 137-142.

Howard, J. S., Sparkman, C. R., Cohen, H.G., Green, G., & Stanislaw, H. (2005). A comparison of intensive behavior analytic and eclectic treatments for young children with autism. *Research in Developmental Disabilities, 26,* 359-383.

Lovaas, O.I. (1987). Behavioral treatment and normal educational functioning in young autistic children. *Journal of Consulting and Clinical Psychology, 55,* 3-9.

Maurice, C. (1993). *Let me hear your voice: A family's triumph over autism.* New York, NY: Knopf.

Maurice, C., Green, G., & Luce, S.C. (Eds.) (1996). *Behavioral intervention for young children with autism: A manual for parents and professionals.* Austin, TX: Pro-Ed.
    This book includes a useful chapter by Psychologist Gina Green on evaluating research.

Sallows, G. O. & Graupner, T. D. (2005). Intensive behavioral treatment for children with autism: Four-year outcome and predictors. *American Journal on Mental Retardation, 110,* 417-438.

Smith, T., Groen, A. D., & Wynn, J. W. (2000). Randomized trial of intensive early intervention for children with pervasive developmental disorders. *American Journal on Mental Retardation,105,* 269-28

McEachin, J.J., Smith, T., & Lovaas, O.I. (1993). Long-term outcome for children with autism who received early intensive behavioral treatment. *American Journal on Mental Retardation, 97,* 359-372.

A good journal to read in order to keep up with new research developments in autism is:

Journal of Autism and Developmental Disorders. You can get information about subscriptions from Springer at their website: www.springerlink.com

3 | Models for Serving Children and Parents

Choosing a Program

Patrick and Mary O'Brien's son, Mike, was diagnosed with autistic disorder a few months before his third birthday and they were advised to seek a good program in applied behavior analysis for their son as quickly as possible. The social worker with whom they met at the child diagnostic center urged them to make immediate contact with their local school district because Mike would be eligible for services from them as soon as he turned three.

The good news was that the O'Briens lived in a community that had opened a special preschool class for children on the autism spectrum a few years ago and had a well staffed and effective program operating. They had a Board Certified Behavior Analyst who consulted to the head teacher, and the teacher herself was nearly finished taking the course work that would make her eligible to sit for the BCBA national examination. The school offered one-to-one instruction for children who needed that intensity and they also had an integrated preschool class where the children with autism spent the day alongside typical peers.

There was also a private preschool for children with autism in a nearby community that had a similar program. The private school had some advantages, including a more intensive home support component and a third classroom that fell between the one-to-one class and the integrated preschool class, offering students a more gradual transition to a group setting. There was also a university-based program about a half hour away from the O'Briens' home, but it was a greater distance *than they wanted their son to travel. Finally, there were some private service providers who would come into the O'Briens' home and work with Mike there for a number of hours each day.*

Both Patrick and Mary worked, so the home-based option was not very appealing to them. Their local school district had also made it clear that they would not pay for the private services or the university-based school, as they believed their public school program was very appropriate and offered the least restrictive setting for Mike. Although they felt some regret about losing the private school option, the O'Briens also recognized that the school district had indeed created a strong program and that it had the advantage of being in the same building where they hoped Mike would go to kindergarten.

How Do Your Choices Compare to the O'Brien Family's?

The O'Briens were fortunate. They lived in an area that was blessed with a relative wealth of resources for serving children with autism. There were public school programs, private school programs, and a university program. There were service providers who would conduct treatment in the home and programs located in schools and other facilities. Although all of them described themselves as "behavioral," some were more faithful to that description than others. This range of services reflects the fact that we do not yet have enough research data to be certain about which models of service delivery are the best, or whether one model is in fact better than another. As a result, the O'Briens, like countless other families, must trust their own judgment.

Models of Intervention

This chapter describes some of the common approaches to the use of behavioral techniques in early intensive intervention for children with autism. We will use specific well-known, highly respected schools as examples of these programs. These programs are located all around the United States and vary greatly in their structure. But they also have common features that make them all excellent. They are not, of course, the only excellent programs available. There are many programs that serve children with autism well; we happen to be most familiar with the ones we talk about here.

Common Features of Excellence

The common features that tie very good early intervention programs together are as important to know as the features that make them different. There are areas of focus that appear again and again in the descriptions of model programs. These include such factors as a rich ratio of adults to children, opportunities for integration with typically developing peers, careful planning for the transition from the specialized program to a more normalized program, opportunities for family involvement, and a well-developed curriculum. It is these common features, summarized in Table 3-1 on the next page, that you can look for when you evaluate specific programs for your child.

Number of Adults

It is not uncommon for programs to offer a one-to-one ratio of adults to children during the child's first year or two of instruction. Although not every excellent program does this, most do. When they

---

Table 3-1 | Some Common Features of Excellent
              Preschool Programs

- ◆ Rich Ratio of Adults to Children
- ◆ Provision for Interaction with Typical Peers
- ◆ Systematic Transition to New Settings
- ◆ Support for Family Involvement
- ◆ Well-Developed Curriculum
- ◆ Sophisticated Knowledge of Applied Behavior Analysis
- ◆ Well-Trained and Well-Supervised Staff
- ◆ Knowledgeable Administrators

do not offer one-to-one teaching, the rationale for doing so is well-developed and not simply the result of insufficient resources.

Access to Typical Peers

At some point in treatment, most excellent programs include an opportunity for contact with typically developing peers. The methods of doing this vary, with some programs offering integrated placement from the child's first days, and others delaying this placement until the child has mastered what they regard as prerequisite skills. Some programs have children with a range of disabilities and include the children with autism in classes for children with other challenges such as learning disabilities or communication delays. Regardless of when they offer integration with typically developing children, excellent programs recognize that for most children with autism, having this exposure in the preschool years is crucial if the child is to achieve full educational integration.

Planned Transition

Administrators of excellent programs have learned that the child will suffer if they do not plan carefully for moves from one class to another, or one school to another. They all therefore make special provisions for working with the teachers who will receive the child in his next placement and for ensuring that the child has the skills needed in the new setting. For example, this process may involve phasing the child into the new classroom during the spring so that he is ready for that class the following fall, doing a careful study of the expectations that are held for children in the class, and ensuring that the child has those skills before the move is completed. The excellent programs will usually offer to follow up as a consultant to the new teacher. It is also common practice to send a well-trained adult with the child to oversee his transition into the new setting.

Supporting Family Involvement

Although parents are important in the education of any child, this is especially true for children with autism. We know it is essential that parents be able to support the teaching that goes on in the classroom. Most parents can become very skilled in behavioral teaching, but they do need the opportunity to practice these methods under the direction of an experienced trainer. All excellent programs recognize the crucial role played by parents and solicit their full involvement. These programs also recognize that, although their teaching staff is expert in behavioral technology, parents are expert in the behavior of their child. It is the combination of these two sources of expertise that will create the best possible outcome for the child.

A Well-Developed Curriculum

The skills to be taught to a child and the sequencing of that instruction are not a matter of random choice. An excellent program should have a well-developed curriculum that includes detailed instructions to teachers about how to teach the specific lessons that are selected. This curriculum is usually carefully sequenced, with an appreciation of the order in which skills need to be learned. In addition, skills are broken down into their many component parts and taught systematically. The features of a well-developed curriculum are discussed more fully in Chapter Five.

Some Exemplary Programs

The programs described in this section are excellent examples of their model. That does not mean they are the only programs adopting that particular model, nor that they are the only excellent ones. We selected these programs either because of their excellent national reputation or because they are ones with which we are familiar. Not being on this list is not a negative reflection on a program. There are countless other excellent choices around the country.

A Public School Program: Lancaster and Lebanon Counties

The Lancaster-Lebanon Intermediate Unit 13 Early Intervention program provides a wide variety of special education preschool services to children with developmental delays across Lancaster and Lebanon Counties in Pennsylvania. Within this early education system, there are six Preschool Autism Support (PAS) classes. Two of the PAS classes run full days, Monday through Friday. The other four PAS classes consist of back-to-back half-day sessions, four days per week. As a general rule, enrollment is limited to six children per class, although at times class size may be expanded to eight, dependent upon student needs and classroom availability. Therefore, up to 48 children can be served within the PAS classes. The staff for each class includes a special education teacher, a "lead trainer," and various paraprofessional instructors. The full-day classes are staffed at near a 1:1 student-to-staff ratio. The half-day classes are less robust in terms of staffing but still allow for a substantial amount of intensive teaching coupled with small group activities.

All methodologies used are based upon axioms of applied behavior analysis, and ongoing data collection allows for data-based decision-making when assessing the efficacy of instruction. The speech-language therapist and occupational therapist assigned to each classroom work with the students in the classroom, working directly with children on goals in their individual IEPs. Two special education consultants are assigned to the classes, including one who is a Board Certified Behavior Analyst. There is ongoing communication with parents via daily logs, phone calls, and parent conferences. Various parent training opportunities are periodically available as well.

Children on the autism spectrum who do not require the intensive instruction and structure of the PAS classes are also served by the Intermediate Unit, either in more traditional special education preschool classes, via consultative support in their typical preschool settings, or within home-based programs.

A University Based Program: Douglass Developmental Disabilities Center

The School Program at the DDDC is based at Rutgers University. It includes three classes for preschool-aged children. There is an entry level preschool class of four children receiving one-to-one instruction. Children with more advanced skills attend the "Small Group" class composed of six children with autism with three or four staff. This class helps the children make the shift from a one-to-one ratio to

working in small groups with other children with autism. In "Small Wonders," the integrated preschool class, six children with autism and seven typically developing peers share a classroom and the attention of four or five adults. There is only a small amount of one-to-one teaching, with most work done in small or large groups.

A speech-language specialist is assigned half time to each preschool class at the DDDC. Parents are provided with training in behavioral techniques. There are regular home visits by support staff to develop home programs. Parents attend conferences at the school along with the full professional staff to share information and make plans for the child. Transitions from class to class and from the preschool to the next placement are carefully planned and usually involve several months of systematic skill building.

A Private School: The Princeton Child Development Institute

Located in Princeton, New Jersey, the Institute is a private special education school serving children and adolescents with autism across the age spectrum. A significant number of the students are of preschool age. Typically, a staff member works with one or two children at a time. The preschool students do not stay in one classroom all day. Rather, the children make many transitions each day from one room to another, from one staff member to another, and to different activities. The rationale underlying these many changes is to maximize the child's opportunities to transfer skills to new environments.

After children have mastered important prerequisite skills at the Institute, they make the transition into more settings with typical peers. This may begin with a day camp or playgroup and then move toward membership in a regular kindergarten or first grade. Family involvement is tailored to the needs of each family.

An early intervention program, opened in 1997, serves children who are 24 months of age or younger at enrollment. In partnership, parents and professionals provide 15 hours of center-based intervention and 20 hours of home-based intervention per week.

A University-Based School: The Walden Preschool

The Walden Preschool is a program for preschool children with autism based at Emory University in Atlanta, Georgia. The model used at Walden is different from that of the other programs described thus far. A ratio of one adult to three children is typical, with a lead teacher and four or five assistants in each class. The emphasis in the Walden program is on social integration, with children with autism and their typically developing peers being part of the same classroom from the early days of the child's enrollment. There is a strong emphasis on teaching the children how to interact with one another. Effective integration also requires careful planning by the teacher and thoughtful arrangement of the classroom and the materials.

The Walden program relies heavily on incidental teaching as opposed to more highly structured Discrete Trial Instruction (DTI). In incidental teaching situations, the teacher tries to create interesting settings that will attract the child's attention and then capitalizes on the child's interests to convey information. For example, if a child picks up a truck, the teacher might comment on its color or shape and ask the child a simple question. She might then encourage the child to push the truck to the garage. In a discrete trial format, the teacher structures the materials and lesson, rather than following the child's lead. The Walden staff encourages parent involvement and provides support for parents in learning the necessary skills. Like the other behavioral programs described in this chapter, the Walden program systematically assesses the children's progress.

A Home-Based University Service: Douglass Outreach Division

One of the services of the Douglass Outreach Division at the DDDC is home-based intervention. Staff members travel to the homes of individual families in New Jersey to provide intensive behavioral intervention. A Program Coordinator is assigned to each family and provides initial training in the principles of applied behavior analysis for the family and other team members. The

Program Coordinator visits the family for a minimum of two hours per week and is responsible for clinical oversight of the program as well as scheduling hours and future training of all team members. In addition, the Program Coordinator supervises all team members, maintains data and records in order to assess progress, makes decisions about educational programming, reports on the student's progress in a written report approximately every three months, and leads monthly meetings for team members and the family.

Instructional time focuses on increasing communication, independence, and choice as well as skills that will increase the child's ability to transition to other less restrictive environments. Staff carefully plan for such transitions, which only occur after a period of systematic skill building.

Team members known as Consultant/Tutors provide direct instruction during sessions structured in two-hour blocks. Families receive a minimum of 10 hours of services a week, and some families with larger teams receive up to 30 hours a week of services. In addition, members of the immediate and extended family often work with their own child for additional hours. The majority of children on the autism spectrum need help with speech and language and Speech-language therapists are available if families should want those services from Douglass Outreach.

In addition to providing preschool services, Douglass Outreach opened an early intervention program in 2005 that currently serves up to thirteen children under the age of three in a home-based setting.

Who Are the People Who Will Serve Your Family?

A variety of professionals may be involved in the treatment of your child. Table 3-2 summarizes information about the credentials and roles of some of the most commonly encountered professionals. The following discussion offers a bit more detail about the role of each professional group listed in the table.

Table 3-2 | Professionals Who May Serve Your Family

Board Certified Behavior Analyst. A Board Certified Behavior Analyst (BCBA) is a person trained in the theory and application of principles of learning. He or she must complete 5 courses in ABA, have many hours of supervised practice, and pass a national examination. People with this credential can come from many disciplines, mainly education, speech and language, and psychology, but other backgrounds are possible. See our comments about "Home Consultants."

Physicians. Pediatricians, family practitioners, child neurologists, developmental pediatricians, and child psychiatrists are among the specialists who can provide medical services including diagnosis of the pervasive developmental disorders, medication for seizures or behavior problems, and ongoing support for your child's health. Each of these medical specialists has an M.D. degree or sometimes a D.O. (Doctor of Osteopathic Medicine) and post graduate training in his or her specialty.

Psychologists. Clinical and school psychologists may provide services to your child including evaluation, diagnosis, consultation to parents and teachers about management of behavior problems, and supervision of the use of behavioral treatments. Psychologists have at least a master's degree and often a doctorate in their specialty.

Teachers. Special education and early childhood education teachers who serve your child have at least a bachelor's degree and often a master's degree in education. They will also be licensed or certified by the state. Teachers are in charge of the classroom in which your child is placed or may work in the home of individual families. In a school setting, the teacher will decide on the programs to be used in teaching your child and will supervise the assistants who work in the class.

Speech-Language Specialists. Speech-language specialists have at least a bachelor's degree and often a master's degree. They may also have a specialty certificate showing their competence. A speech-language specialist is often part of a child's treatment team in a school setting.

Home Consultants. Home consultants are people who come to the home of a child with autism to set up and supervise a behavioral program for the child. Consultants can have any academic degree or none at all. Because there are no laws about credentials or degrees required for this role, the quality of people who offer these services is highly variable.

Physicians

Your first professional contact when you were seeking information about your child's autism was probably with the pediatrician or family practitioner who takes care of your child's overall health. These medical specialists are physicians who have completed medical school and have done specialty training as well. It is not uncommon for a pediatrician or family practitioner to refer parents to a specialist who has more experience with developmental disorders in order to obtain a diagnosis from an expert.

One common referral is to a pediatric neurologist. This physician has training in both neurology (study of how the brain works) and pediatrics, and specializes in disorders of the nervous system that occur in children. Another common referral for a diagnosis would be to a developmental pediatrician. This is a pediatrician who specializes in problems of development. Another medical specialist who might have identified your child as having a pervasive developmental disorder is a child psychiatrist. This physician specializes in mental disorders of children. All three specialists would usually have considerable experience in recognizing autism spectrum disorders.

Physicians are valuable in making the initial diagnosis of a pervasive developmental disorder. They can also reevaluate your child over time to assess the progress he is making. If your child needs medication, develops a seizure disorder, or has some other medical problem, a physician will be central in that treatment. However, physicians do not administer intensive behavioral intervention, as it is not a medical treatment. You will be referred to other specialists for that care.

Psychologists

Clinical and school psychologists are often involved in the care of children with autism. Clinical psychologists usually have a doctorate (Psy.D. or Ph.D.) in psychology and have done a full-year psychological internship. There are some clinical psychologists with a master's degree. Clinical psychologists specialize in the diagnosis and treatment of psychological disorders. Some of them are expert in the assessment and treatment of autism. School psychologists may have a doctorate or a master's degree. They are trained to work in schools and have special expertise in the assessment and education of children. Most school districts employ school psychologists to evaluate children, consult to teachers, and help parents find a school or particular classroom within a school that will meet their child's educational needs.

A psychologist may play an important role in evaluating your child. For example, he or she might administer special tests of your child's adaptive functioning and test his intelligence. Some psychologists are expert in diagnosis using the Autism Diagnostic Observation Schedule (ADOS; Lord, Rutter, DiLavore, & Risi, 1999) and the Autism Diagnostic Interview-Revised (ADIR; Lord, Rutter, & LeCouteur, 1994). In addition, psychologists are often called upon for consultation when a child is posing behavior problems or does not seem to benefit from treatment. Some psychologists work directly with children with autism or train parents in behavioral techniques. They may also conduct support groups for parents or siblings of children with autism.

Teachers

A teacher may be at the heart of your child's treatment. Teachers have at least a bachelor's degree and may have a master's degree in education. All states require that teachers be certified or licensed by the state as qualified to teach. This may include a specialty credential in special education. Being a certified or licensed teacher does not ensure that a teacher has expertise in treating autism. It is important that any teacher who is working independently with your child have had supervised experience with children with autism and be skilled in the use of ABA teaching methods.

A teacher may be the person who identifies the skills to be learned by your child and teaches these specific lessons to your child. Typically, the teacher of children with autism has one or more

assistants who work under his or her supervision in the classroom, implementing the programs written by the teacher. Because the teacher's role is so vital to your child, it is important that you feel confident about the skills this person brings to the classroom.

Speech-Language Specialist

Variously known as speech-language pathologists, speech therapists, or speech-language specialists, these individuals usually have a master's degree and may have certification from the American Speech-Language-Hearing Association to document their expertise. This special credential is called a Certificate of Clinical Competence in Speech-Language Pathology. If you see the letters CCC-SLP after a speech therapist's name, it means he or she has met high standards of professional competence. Speech therapists can have a variety of specialties. Any speech therapist who works with your child should have had supervised experience in working with children with autism.

These professionals help children who do not yet have language learn basic communication skills, including the use of speech or nonvocal communication with manual signs, pictures, or gestures. When children have some speech, the speech therapist addresses ways to expand on the complexity of the speech and help the child speak more clearly, if articulation is an issue. Increasing sentence length, teaching the child to use conventional language more effectively, using proper intonation, and being clear in his speech would all be goals that a speech and language therapist might address, depending on the child's needs.

Speech and language intervention for children with autism is probably most effective when the teacher and the speech-language specialist collaborate closely. For example, at the Douglass School our speech-language specialists spend many hours a week directly in the classroom. They run language groups, work alongside of the teacher as full partners, and help the staff implement language goals. Like teachers, speech-language specialists will play a central role in your child's treatment.

Other Professionals

Other professionals may also be involved in your child's treatment. A physical therapist, who specializes in helping children with gross motor problems, may provide services if your child has problems with mobility. A school nurse may administer medication a physician prescribes. Some programs employ occupational therapists to help children with specific sensory problems or fine motor skills such as handwriting or using scissors. Social workers may run parent support groups and provide family support.

Para-educators

In addition to the professional staff, there are often para-educational staff who work with the children. These individuals, whose educational backgrounds vary, are trained to carry out specific tasks under professional supervision. For example, a classroom assistant or assistant teacher may conduct teaching sessions with your child, implementing the programs written by the teacher. Many para-educators become highly skilled in their work. At the Douglass Center many of our assistant teachers are people with bachelor's degrees in education or psychology who are working while they continue to go to school for a master's degree. They are usually highly intelligent and devoted people who are very effective. However, there is no credential required in most settings to become a para-educator, and you need to be certain that the people who work in your child's program are well trained and well supervised.

It is possible (and desirable) for an individual working at this level to become Board Certified as an Associate Behavior Analyst (BCABA) if she has a college degree. People with a BCABA should continue to be supervised by a Board Certified Behavior Analyst.

Home Consultants

Home consultants come to the home of the child with autism and attempt to teach the child a broad array of skills, including social skills, language, self-help skills, and the management of disruptive behavior. In many cases, they share this knowledge with parents and support them in carrying out instructional programs for their child.

There are currently no regulations concerning who can provide home-based consultation to parents of children with autism. As a result, a number of people with various levels of competence have "set up shop" offering their services to families. Some of these folks are superb and some may do more harm than good. Sadly, we are aware of children who appear to have been harmed by a consultant who did not know how to create a coherent program for the child. As we have suggested at other places in this book, it is therefore essential that you select a service provider very carefully.

Someone who works independently as a consultant to families should be well trained in the principles of applied behavior analysis. His or her background should include an in-depth knowledge of ABA, a sophisticated understanding of the procedures used to decrease disruptive behavior, a detailed understanding of autism, and a well-developed teaching curriculum. A master's degree or a doctorate in one of the appropriate professions, including psychology, education, or speech would be important, although there are some people with less education but many years of applied experience who offer good services. A formal educational degree by itself is not insurance that a person has the necessary know-how. It is essential that their training have included the skills just described. This knowledge should not be based solely on reading books or sitting in class. It is important that the person have extensive hands-on experience teaching preschool-aged children with autism un-

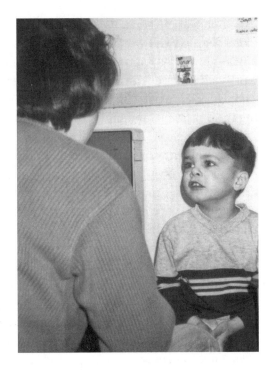

der the direct supervision of someone who is expert in that work.

If a consultant does not have a formal educational background in applied behavior analysis, you need to ensure that he or she has sufficient training to be able to handle all of the many complexities that arise in educating a child with autism. Check their credentials very carefully. When in doubt, shop around.

The best way to ensure that a home consultant has a good academic background in ABA combined with supervised experience is to hire someone who is a Board Certified Behavior Analyst (BCBA). This credential, which requires 15 academic credits and a number of hours of supervision, has become increasingly common in the past decade. However, there are still not enough people with the BCBA to serve every family who needs one. Consequently, it is not uncommon for the person who is a BCBA to directly supervise other people and train them in how to carry out the programs your child needs. These people do not have the breadth of training and experience to develop new programs without close input from the BCBA.

Some home consultation agencies employ people with bachelor's degrees who work under the supervision of individuals with a BCBA or many years of supervised experience. That system can work well if there is an arrangement to ensure close supervision of their work. Find out who is supervising the person who will be coming to your home, and make sure the supervisor is competent and will have an active role in overseeing the work of your consultant. For example, a well-run program does not usually allow the staff member to go on home consultations alone until after he or she has first done many, many visits with a senior staff member.

Initially, the new staff member observes the senior person, and then gradually he or she starts to take responsibility for some aspects of the visits. Before the junior person is allowed to go to a home on his or her own, the supervisor will have observed complete visits during which the staff member took full responsibility for the consultation. Even new people with advanced degrees should go through this procedure. After they are allowed to make independent visits, staff should still meet weekly with their supervisor to review programming concerns. Videotaped reviews can be incorporated into supervision, and senior staff should join consultants on their visits on a periodic basis.

In Sum

Intensive applied behavior analysis is used in a number of different settings. In the absence of good research comparing these various models of service delivery, parents have to use common sense in choosing among programs. When you evaluate a program, be certain you understand such things as the ratio of adults to children, the kind of access children with autism have to typically developing peers, how children are aided in the transition to new settings, and how parents are trained in behavioral methods. If you are contracting for home-based services, pay special attention to the credentials of the person who will serve your family, and to the supervision available to staff within the agency.

Parents Speak

It was really rough in the beginning. My son would be crying downstairs and I would be crying and praying upstairs. I
wondered if I did the right thing. He was so young to have to go
through this torture. But as the weeks passed and the therapy
increased, we began to see results. You live and die by what the
therapist tells you after each session. It was amazing! Little
things he couldn't do before he started to do. I then knew we
were on the right road.

I don't consider myself a very religious person but I do
go to church on Sunday and I do pray daily. I feel God has put
certain people in my life that led me to where I am today. It is
so important when you're dealing with this disorder that the
right people come into your life to help you. My advice to other
parents is to seek outreach services with schools that are well
known in the field of autism.

๑๑

One of the first things that struck me when we walked into
the school was that everyone was busy with kids. They all
seemed to know what they were doing. When we watched
through the one-way mirror, I was really impressed. There
was one adult for every child. And so much energy. I've never
seen adults with so much enthusiasm and warmth. The kids
loved it. You could tell they were happy. That helped me
make up my mind.

๑๑

After the interview I prayed a lot. I knew we had found a place
where Danielle would get help. They said they had to wait to
be certain there was an opening. I kept my fingers crossed. We
had watched the preschool class with all the typical kids and

the ones with autism. I had a hard time telling them apart. I just kept hoping Danielle would be there some day. The miracle is that she finally made it. I don't know what her future will be, but she is doing great right now.

❧

Our son is one of the children who have moved very slowly. He had two years of one-to-one teaching. First he had a year at home and then a year in school. He has made some progress, but he is still very autistic. Next year he will be too old for the preschool and we are looking for the right class for him. He is probably always going to need a lot of help. I knew there were no guarantees, but I kept hoping my son would be one of the lucky ones. It isn't easy.

❧

Overall, in spite of the effectiveness of ABA, it is a bit heart-wrenching to teach your child this way. This is, after all, just a highly refined version of teaching tricks to a dog. But at least in some cases, and in our son's case, it somehow also teaches the brain how to think.

References

Handleman, J.S. & Harris, S. L. (Eds.). (In press). *Preschool education programs for children with autism. 3rd ed.* Austin, TX: Pro-Ed.

    The program descriptions in this chapter were based primarily on this book. It is a readable paperback that parents as well as professionals find useful.

Lord, C., Rutter, M., & LeCouteur, A. (1994). Autism Diagnostic Interview-Revised: A revised version of a diagnostic interview for caregivers of individuals with possible developmental disorders. *Journal of Autism and Developmental Disorders, 24,* 659-685.

Lord, C., Rutter, M., DiLavore, P. C., & Risi, S. (1999). *Autism diagnostic observation schedule - WPS edition (ADOS-WPS).* Los Angeles: Western Psychological Service.

4 | Home-Based, Center-Based, and School-Based Programs

Who Should Teach Our Child?

Alva and Malik Carver decided they wanted to use ABA methods to educate their three-year-old daughter, Evie, who had a diagnosis of autistic disorder. After talking to several families who had home programs and discussing their options, they decided that Alva would take a leave from her job as a nurse practitioner and stay at home with Evie to supervise a home program. Malik made a good living and they had already put away some money for Evie's college education. They decided to use those funds, combined with financial help from each of their families, to fund two years of home-based work. It was now a matter of finding the right professional to supervise the program.

Their next step was going online to the website for the Behavior Analyst Certification Board (www.bacb.com). There they found a registry where they could locate people who held the BCBA (Board Certified Behavior Analyst) certification and who were close to their home town. There were provisions on the website to contact via e-mail people who might be appropriate. They e-mailed several certified professionals who offered home-based services, interviewed two of these people, and settled on one.

Mary Torres, the consultant Alva and Malik selected, had her master's degree in special education and had worked for some years in a center-based program for young children with autism. She had earned her BCBA three years earlier and said she always went to the annual meeting of the Association for Behavior Analysis (www.abainternational.org) to keep up to date. She was open and frank about her training and her experience. Ms. Torres seemed quite knowledgeable about applied behavior analysis and was very much at ease when she worked with Evie. The Carvers knew that as important as having the BCBA credential was, it did not ensure that a consultant had good "people" skills, and they wanted to be certain Mary Torres was good in that domain as well. So, before they committed themselves, they contacted several families with whom Ms. Torres had worked and got rave reviews about her competence. The other parents said she had had a truly professional attitude toward her work and was very effective with their children.

The next step in the consultation process was for Mary Torres to come to the Carvers' home to do an initial workshop. During this first visit, she taught Alva and Malik and their assistants the basics of ABA and gave them a set of teaching programs to do with Evie until the next visit. She helped them set up a quiet space in a corner of the family room where their teaching center would be located. She also emphasized that she would expect to talk to them by telephone at least once a week to help fine tune their programs and wanted to see videotapes on a regular basis.

Although the consultant made suggestions about how to find help, it was up to the family to recruit the tutors who would actually conduct the teaching sessions with their daughter. The Carvers lived close to a community college, which turned out to be a very good source of helpers. They also found two young people in their church who wanted to volunteer their help. Eventually, they identified four people who were interested in psychology or education, who liked small children, and who wanted to learn the instructional methods to be used in the programs for Evie.

Then Alva Carver and Mary Torres trained the students in how to use applied behavior analysis, and these tutors did much of the actual teaching. However, Alva herself spent many hours a week teaching and Malik worked with his daughter on the weekends. It was a demanding schedule, made more complex because the family had a son just two years older than Evie. Meeting the needs of both children was exhausting, and the Carvers worried that they might be neglecting their son. They were, however, very gratified with the progress Evie made. After two months of instruction, their little girl was much easier to manage, was starting to use a few words, and followed a long list of instructions. It was a good start.

Is the Carver Family's Choice Right for Your Family?

A home-based program was the most appealing choice for the Carver family. Although it required considerable financial sacrifice and they had to accept money from both sets of grandparents to make it work, they believed they could adapt their lifestyle for the two years Evie was in the program and that the outcome might be very worthwhile. Other families might have a much less flexible lifestyle or financial needs that preclude having one parent stop working outside the home for two years. The sacrifice might not be feasible. For example, without both parents' income they might have to sell their home.

Many school districts have their own programs for preschool-aged children with autism spectrum disorders and are therefore unwilling to fund a home-based program. As a result, families choosing to implement a home-based program might have to bear the full cost. School-based and centered-based programs are very appropriate options for families who do not have the financial or personal flexibility to set up their own program. Even if a family can afford a home-based program, many people report that the out-of-home options are equally as attractive and hence more appealing. Regardless of the ultimate choice they make, for many families choosing an educational setting is the single most complex choice they face in planning their child's education.

What Setting Is Best for Your Family?

School-based, home-based, and center-based models of treatment are all in widespread use and advocates for all three

approaches report substantial benefits from their efforts. To date, there have been no good research studies comparing these three approaches. Consequently, parents will need to rely on their own good judgment in making this decision. For the Carver family, having a great deal of daily involvement was central to their choice of a home-based program. For another family, the availability of an excellent school-based or center-based program could determine their preference. For almost every family, finances play an important role. Geography is also a factor. Some families in rural areas, far from a school-based or center-based program, may find a home-based program their best option.

Making Choices

There are a number of factors to consider in making the choice among a home-based, school-based, and center-based program. This chapter first provides a brief description of each model and then reviews some of the pros and cons of each approach. Table 4-1 summarizes some of these factors.

Table 4-1 | Factors to Consider in Home-Based,
School-Based, and Center-Based Programs

- The Time Demands on Parents
- Degree of Parental Control over the Child's Educational Program
- Access to Multidisciplinary Team
- Availability of Experienced Teaching Staff
- Time Spent by the Child in Travel
- Time Spent in Required Activities
- Influence of Visual and Auditory Distractions
- The Availability of Typically Developing Peers
- The Age Appropriate Nature of Being at Home
- Impact on Family Finances

Home-Based Treatment

The term "home-based" refers to a treatment program that occurs, at least initially, within the child's own home. A room of the house, perhaps the child's bedroom or a family recreation room, is selected as the work area. Ideally the room should be relatively distraction free, with attractive items such as toys or video games out of sight and out of reach except when the trainer wants to offer them to the child. Small tables, chairs, beanbag chairs, a carpeted floor, and instructional materials are conveniently located so that the child's tutors can have easy access to them.

In the home-based model, parents contract with a professional service provider to come to their home to oversee their child's educational program. Sometimes this professional is a consultant who only visits the family periodically, and other times the consultant may do a large portion of the instruction with the child, as well as oversee the curriculum and train other team members. When the professional consults on a periodic basis, the family will typically take the initiative to find other team members who actually run the programs developed by the consultant. These team members may be volunteers from the community or individuals who are paid for their services. Regardless of the consultant's level of involvement,

the parents themselves are almost always part of the team who are responsible for the child's education.

Finding good tutors is a task in itself. Among the most helpful places to look are the psychology, speech, and special education departments of colleges and universities, and churches, synagogues, and other volunteer groups. College students tend to be very bright, idealistic, and hard working. Those are excellent qualities to look for in a tutor! You can call a college and ask them to post notices describing the job and you can place a help wanted ad in the campus paper. You can also ask your priest, rabbi, minister, etc. how to recruit volunteers from your place of worship.

Although using volunteers will save you money, it is not easy to find enough to people to fill a child's schedule. In addition, paying people may make you more comfortable about making demands on them. A good way to find out what the appropriate rate of payment is for your own community is to ask other families who are employing home-based practitioners. You can also find out what organizations within your community pay their staff members who serve in a similar role.

After a child with autism has made sufficient progress within the home, steps are taken to provide exposure to other children. This can be arranged through playgroups, summer day camps, other recreational groups, and nursery school or day care settings. Ultimately, if the treatment goes well, the child would be moved into a regular education setting such as kindergarten or first grade.

Even if a child has made only moderate progress in a home-based program during the preschool years, it is important that she be given the opportunity to learn in a school-based setting rather than remaining within the home. Older children need to learn to function in a broader setting, whether in the public schools or more specialized schools. With rare exceptions, that means that once a child has completed preschool, her only home-based work should occur after school or on weekends, and she should spend the school day with peers of her own age.

Center-Based Treatment

Center-based treatment usually occurs in a specialized school, although it might be done in a classroom, a hospital clinic, or early intervention center. Although some school districts will fund this specialized opportunity, others will not and it may fall to the family to pay for the experience.

The same ABA techniques that are used in a home-based program can be used in a center-based one. Most center-based programs expect families to provide support for their work by carrying out some instructional programs in the home. However, the time demands on parents involved in center-based programs are more modest than for those involved in home-based programs.

Many center-based programs provide one-to-one treatment for very young children and then gradually move them on to small group and larger group experiences. Children often spend five or six hours a day in this setting, and over the course of the day may work with several staff members including certified teachers, assistant teachers, speech and language specialists, and adaptive physical education instructors. The proximity of the treatment team and the relative ease of coordination among them is a major advantage of a center-based program. Children in center-based programs, like those in home-based programs, are usually systematically introduced to settings where they can interact with typically developing peers.

School-Based Programs

There is considerable overlap between center-based and school-based programs. However we are distinguishing the school-based program as one that operates in a public school setting with all of the advantages that implies. Not least of these is if your child is determined to be eligible for services through one of these programs, they will be provided at no cost to you.

In the past decade, many school districts around the country have elected to create their own school-based program for children with autism. These programs resemble center-based programs in many respects with the added advantage of easy access to peers for inclusion activities. They may not, however, always have the intensity of treatment offered in home- or center-based programs. Depending on the school system, your child may be offered fewer hours per week of treatment than she would get in a home-based or center-based program or there might be less one-on-one time with teachers. It is important to explore in depth the extent of the services that will be provided to your child in your local community.

The Pros and Cons

All three models, home-, center-, and school-based, have advantages and disadvantages. Taking these factors into account may help you decide about which direction you prefer to go and which is realistic for your family.

Demands on Parents

In a home-based model, parents have the primary responsibility for coordinating their child's education. They may be responsible for a significant portion of the child's direct instruction. Even if they have a full cadre of helpers to do most of the teaching, the parents typically coordinate everyone's efforts, train new team members, and ensure that everyone is working on the same tasks in the same fashion. Their home consultant provides them with instructional programs and ensures that the child is making good progress in a well-developed instructional sequence. The home consultant also trains the parents and the tutors in the teaching methods.

Because of the high degree of responsibility for their child's education, parents who use a home-based model must be very skilled in using applied behavior analysis and able to make day-by-day decisions about their child's progress within programs. By contrast, in a school- or center-based program, the child's teacher usually plays the role of coordinator and supervisor. The teacher, who typically has a degree in special education and may also be certified in early childhood education, has back-up support from a team of professional consultants. Although parents play a crucial role in ensuring that material taught in a center-based model is transferred to the home and to the child's regular routine, this is far less daunting for most parents than being the person with primary instructional responsibility.

The home-based model works best in families where one parent can remain at home to oversee the child's progress. That usually rules out the use of this model in families where both parents must work to support the family. When one parent does stay home, it is most often mothers who oversee their child's program. However, we know several fathers who supervise their child's home program.

Among the factors that parents take into account in deciding which parent will stay home are the personalities of the parents, their ability to tolerate the demands of the task, and the income-earning potential of each partner. For example, in one family we know the mother is a highly paid attorney and the father a more modestly compensated high school guidance counselor. They decided it would be easier to live on the mother's income and have the father stay home rather than vice versa. They also commented to us that the father was a slower-paced, more relaxed person who could adapt more readily to being home full time than could the mother. Each family using a home-based program needs to consider these sorts of factors in deciding who will remain at home and who will work outside of the home.

Grandparents, aunts, uncles, and other family members may sometimes play a central role in the education of a child with autism. For example, they may act as one of the child's "tutors." Rarely, they may be the person who coordinates a child's instruction. However, because it is a time-consuming role that requires a great deal of control and decision-making about the child, asking a close family member or a good friend to assume this supervisory role may complicate the relationships in a family. Therefore, you should think carefully about how this arrangement would fit in your own circumstances.

Sometimes parents have little if any choice about taking on the primary instructional role for their child. For example, if you live in an isolated area where there are few resources, your only option may be to rely on home-based teaching. Your consultant might live in a large city and fly in to see you on a regular basis. Similarly, if you live in a country where no one knows much about teaching children with autism, you have to take on a central role in your child's instruction because no one else knows how. Some families outside of the United States, Canada, Australia, and Western Europe rely on a home-based consultation model for their child.

For most single-parent families or for families in which both parents must work, the home-based model is not feasible. There also are some families who are facing multiple crises such as the illness of a grandparent, a parent, or another child. As a result of these circumstances they cannot devote the amount of time required for a home-based program. For these families, a center- or school-based program is the better option.

Parental Control Over the Child's Education

The concept of parental involvement is a sword that cuts two ways. Home-based programs require more parent involvement than do center- or school-based programs, but they also give parents more complete control over their child's education. The parents are the ones who call all the shots. Many parents who use a home-based approach are superbly skilled in applied behavior analysis. They also know their child's personality more intimately than any professional could. As a result, these parents are in an excellent position to make day-by-day and often minute-by-minute decisions about their child's progress on a particular instructional sequence. Because they love their child and are most deeply invested in her welfare, they may be ideal advocates and teachers for her.

In a center- or school-based program, parents inevitably surrender some control to the professional staff. In a good program, when both parents and professionals are open to one another's ideas, that sharing can result in a smoothly running program in which there is a sense of common goals and mutual respect. Most quality programs have liberal arrangements for visits by parents. This gives parents the opportunity to observe the teaching methods that are being used and enhances the communication between parents and professional staff members. Under these conditions, multiple partners can all contribute to the child's learning, and the family and child will benefit from that network of support. This collaborative approach does, however, place demands on all of the participants to learn to voice their opinions and concerns, listen carefully to one another, and be flexible in their approach.

In lower quality programs, there may be less respect for a parent's perspective and professionals may not be so attuned to the family's needs. In these cases, there is usually less communication, which can result in frustration for both parties and a diminishing of the child's educational experience. Good communication must go beyond the formal IEP meetings to allow a sharing of on-going concerns and achievements around the child's learning experiences.

Parents and professionals both share the burden of learning how to collaborate. Although it is part of school personnel's job to listen with respect and care to parents, that listening and respect is a two-way street. Parents can support and encourage teaching staff, and recognize that they too have their vulnerabilities and needs that may intrude on their objectivity. It is in the best interests of the child when all of the partners are willing to work at effective communication.

The Availability of a Multidisciplinary Team

Center-based programs typically have a group of autism professionals available for consultation and service. Usually this group includes speech-language specialists, who have expertise in language development, and psychologists, who can consult on the management of behavior problems and who understand the theory underlying applied behavior analysis as well as how to do and understand research. Depending on your child's individual needs, other professionals, including physicians, physical therapists, and occupational therapists, may also be called on for consultation. Although these same professionals might also be called on for school-based consultations, they are less likely to be found on staff as full-time autism experts, as most school districts may not have enough children with autism to justify that full-time investment. In many school systems, the on-staff professionals are generalists who know something about many childhood problems, but who are not always steeped in the study of autism.

When a child is in a home-based program, these additional services need to be sought out individually, and they might not be as easily coordinated as in a center-based program, where staff routinely talk with one another. That coordination among professionals becomes another task for the family. Although some insurance plans may provide reimbursements for at least some of the services a child receives, many others do not. That leaves it up to the school district or the family to cover the expenses. In addition, parents may need to travel with their child to the offices of these professionals for services.

The Use of Experienced Team Members

Centers also have considerable "depth of talent" because their primary focus is on the education of children with autism. A school-based program which has only one or two classes for children on the autism spectrum may have to hire outside experts to consult on an as-needed basis and the classroom teacher may be the only autism expert present on a daily basis. In an established center-based

program there are a group of trained staff who are intimately familiar with the ABA procedures that have been shown to be helpful in educating children with autism. These are usually full-time staff members who are familiar with behavioral technology, have been extensively supervised in its application, and may have their BCBA. Home-based programs often make use of nonprofessional tutors who must be trained before they are ready to work with the child. Even after training, these tutors need considerable on-going supervision.

Time Spent in Transportation

In a home-based program, the staff comes to the child, while in a center- or school-based program the child travels to the program. Time spent in travel is time not spent in instruction, and if a child has a long trip to the center or school, this can add up to a considerable part of the day. In addition, if the school district does not pay for the center-based program, it may fall to the parents to transport their child. On the other hand, a number of parents have commented to us that their child naps on the bus on the way home, and arrives at the door full of new energy and ready to go. This issue of time spent in travel is a very individual one.

Time Spent in Required Activities

Center- and school-based programs often have a number of required activities including nap time, lunch breaks, fire drills, and the like. These events may not be attuned to the needs of the individual child. On the other hand, these kinds of events are part of the normal routine of childhood and it is useful for a child to learn how to handle them. In a home-based program, breaks can be taken as the child needs them, and less total time is consumed when only one child needs to be taken to the toilet, fed lunch, and so forth.

The Influence of Visual and Auditory Distractions

Classrooms are often noisy places. Bring two or more children together in a small space and there will be noise. In center- and school-based programs, children may be doing their one-to-one work in a small classroom where there are other adults and children working as well. The sounds and the sights of other people may be distracting to some young children with autism. One child's laughter or tantrum may distract another child's concentration. On the other hand, such distractions are part of the natural environment for every child, and the child with autism will have to learn to cope with the presence of others if she is going to function in a more typical setting.

At the Douglass Center, we reduce the distractions for our youngest students by working with each child in an individual cubby. In a home-based program, an environment can be created that is essentially distraction free. Eventually the child will have to be weaned from that level of quiet to a more normalized setting, but for some young children, beginning with a distraction-free setting can be helpful.

Ease of Access to Typically Developing Peers

Regardless of whether a child is in a home-, school-, or center-based program, it is important to provide contact with typically developing peers. In a center-based program, there is often a ready-made procedure for creating this opportunity. The peers may be enrolled in the same school or even the same class, or there may be an arrangement with a nearby public school to offer that integrated experience. It is even easier in a school-based program, where most of the children in the building are typically developing youngsters. Families using home-based programs often have to make their own arrangements to integrate their child with typically developing peers and then directly supervise that integration.

The Age of the Child

Many typically developing young children spend their entire day at home. Although less common than it was a couple of generations ago, it is still not unusual for the parent of a preschool-aged child to be home full-time with that child. The use of a home-based program in the early years is therefore consistent in some ways with the amount of time that a parent might give to a typically developing child.  However, in our contemporary western society, children who are approaching school age usually have some sort of social experience beyond the home. In most cases it would be highly artificial for an older child with autism to be isolated from her same-age peers.

The Impact on Family Finances

As of this writing, the cost of running a good home-based program of 35 to 40 hours a week can range between $40,000 and

$100,000 a year in U.S. dollars. Of course, if you rely primarily on family and volunteers, it will cost less than if you hire several professionals to work with your child. Given that many families lack the personal funds and/or the time to do this work, it is typically the role of the school district to pay for the services.

Not every school district will readily agree to a home-based program. They are expensive to provide, and if there are several preschool-aged children with autism in a community, it may not be cost-effective to educate each child in his or her own home. Some schools may resist home-based programs because they are not the "least restrictive environment." It may help in these cases to remind the school personnel that very young children often remain at home with their parents, and that home is the most "natural" environment for a small child. In addition, you could point out that the home setting does not have many of the visual and auditory distractions that can be a problem for children with autism in a school setting. However, if the school district has an adequate program of their own, they may very well resist these and other arguments with the counter claim that they have an appropriate and least restrictive setting.

Persuading a School District to Fund Services. Some parents who are committed to the value of the home-based model have turned to litigation to pressure a school system to provide the funds to support a home-based program. Sometimes the family prevails in these legal proceedings and sometimes the school district prevails. There is no assurance that a lawsuit will result in obtaining a home-based program. Some affluent families may be able to pay the educational bill themselves, but home-based programs of the level of intensity and behavioral sophistication necessary to provide appropriate treatment are very expensive. Unless an outside agency pays the bill, it may be impossible for most families to have access to this service.

If you live in a community that has no suitable resources for the education of preschool-aged children with autism, there are some strategies you can use to try to persuade your school district to pay for a home-based program including the cost of tutors and consultants, or to create a high quality school-based program within the district:

1. Help the district professionals become aware of the empirical support available for the use of applied behavior analysis. Pointing out the research studies and sharing books such as ours may help the members of the child study team understand why this treatment is so vital.

2. If you are already using these methods at home, you may want to videotape sessions of your child being taught by the use of applied behavior analysis. You could tape one of the very first sessions when your child may have been resistant and difficult, and then a session a little later when she has become cooperative and responsive.

3. If your child hasn't started using ABA yet, you might use the videotapes made by Ivar Lovaas and Ronald Leaf (available through Pro-Ed) to illustrate the benefits of ABA treatment.

4. Showing data on your child's mastery of new skills, or data from another child's program, if your child hasn't begun a program, would be a good way to document how she benefits from the teaching approach. You might also contrast your child's progress using applied behavior analysis with her progress in previous teaching attempts.

If you're interested in having your child participate in a program even though it's out of your school district, the staff at the program might be able to help you with arguments to persuade your school district to send your child there. They might also be willing to speak to officials from your school district about what's involved in setting up and maintaining such a program. Finally, have a consultant in applied behavior analysis come to the IEP or IFSP meeting to speak directly with the team members about the teaching methods.

Even if your district is adamant about not paying for your home program, they may still be willing to pay for related services such as speech and language therapy. Do take advantage of every opportunity they offer as long as the methods being used in these related services are compatible with your home-based program.

It may make sense to take the services your school district is willing to provide, and combine them with services you can afford to provide. Many families prove their child with a blend of services. For example, the child may go to a school-based program for 20 hours a week, and have home-based instruction for another 20, of which 10 might be done by parents. If you elect this format it will usually fall to you as a parent to ensure that the instructional methods and materials that are being used are compatible across settings so that your child does not become confused by contradictory methods of instruction.

Finally, if data, logic, and the law all fail you in your efforts to establish the kind of center-, school-, or home-based program your child requires, use every ounce of creativity to get the resources your child needs. Remember, the best gains are made by children who start a program of intensive behavioral intervention early. Do what you must to get this help. That can include setting up your own program, moving to another community where better services are available, recruiting volunteers, going to the newspaper with your story, and so forth.

In Sum

The choice among home-based, school-based, and center-based programs is not always clear cut. A number of factors should be weighed in making a decision for your child. These include the quality of the center-based and school-based programs available in your community, the resources available for home-based instruction, and your family's needs. At our own center, we offer both home-based and center-based services to ensure that families have a choice of services. Since there are no good data documenting that one model is superior, the most important thing to evaluate is the competency of the professionals who offer the services. In center-based and school-based programs, you generally have some assurance of competency because staff members are typically accountable to a supervisor. However, while the BCBA is gaining increasing acceptance, in most areas there are presently no credential requirements for home-based consultants, and anyone who wishes can claim to be an expert and offer his or her services. When it comes to home-based programs, that old adage "Let the buyer beware" is a sound warning. You owe it to your child to be a well-informed consumer.

Parents Speak

Running a home-based program can be very hard on your family life. Depending on how many hours per week you have therapy, it puts a strain financially and mentally on the family. Our lives revolved around our son's therapy schedule. I was also involved with hiring therapists, making up their schedules, and trying to rearrange sessions when they couldn't keep their appointment time. When I couldn't get someone to fill in, I was so frustrated. He wasn't getting the therapy he so desperately needed and I wasn't getting the free time I so desperately needed. I also have a seven-year-old son who needs me too and I always have to arrange his schedule around his brother's.

Having the home-based program was working great. He was making tremendous progress and was changing into a different little boy. However, it was time for him to go to school. As much as I hate to admit it—we both needed a break from each other. I wanted him to go to a school that had the intensive program he had at home and I wanted him to start to develop social skills. If he was ever going to be mainstreamed some day, he would need those skills. Putting my baby on that bus at age three was the hardest thing I ever had to do. I cried so hard when he waved goodbye that first day. Fortunately, he loves going on the bus so it makes it much easier for me to let go.

☙❧

The home-based program was terrific. Our daughter made good progress and we always knew what was going on. But, it came at a big price. I had to quit my job and my husband ended up working overtime almost every night. We had to take out a second mortgage too. For more than a year we hardly saw each other. When the weekends came, we were both exhausted. This year she is in a regular first grade class, but she still needs a lot of help. I'm not sure how this is going to work out. I do know that without the home-based program she might not have gone anywhere. We don't have any special autism programs in our community and I really needed the help I got. Our therapists were great.

Most of the people who have helped our son have been wonderful. But in the beginning we interviewed someone who was a loser. She told us she could set up a complete program for our son, train our tutors and us, and develop the curriculum. When we checked her references, we found out her only training was six months as an assistant in a classroom. Parents need to be careful who they hire.

I knew from the beginning that we wanted Tim in a school. My husband and I both work and we couldn't stop. I guess we're lucky because there are great schools in our state and we got Tim into one that uses applied behavior analysis. Plus, the school district was great. They worked with us every step of the way. The school psychologists told us they know that if Tim gets a good start now it will be best for him and probably save the taxpayers thousands of dollars too.

Home programming is essential. Children with autism won't succeed if they get mixed messages. What's done at school must also be done at home.

We have begun scaling back on his home therapy and filling the time with organized activities. In particular, two months ago we enrolled him in karate school. The instructors were not told that he had a problem and so far no one has asked.

Reference

The Lovaas Learning Videotapes (Lovaas & Leaf), can be ordered from Pro-Ed. Their address is 8700 Shoal Creek Blvd., Austin, TX 78757-6897. 800-397-7633. www.proedinc.com.

5 | What to Teach and How to Teach It: Curriculum and Teaching Programs

The Horowitz Family

Lou and Elaine Horowitz knew that their son Max needed intensive help, and they knew that they wanted him to have ABA intervention. When Max was 18 months, the parents had pleaded with their pediatrician to refer them to a specialist, as they felt he was far behind where his brother had been at that age. At first, early interventionists had helped with his motor and speech skills, and he had made substantial progress. Then it became clear that he would need early intensive behavioral intervention, as his autism spectrum issues became more apparent. Lou and Elaine knew that Max had deficits in many areas and would need extensive help, but they could not quite imagine how a program would try to address all of those needs from a teaching perspective.

One of the biggest problems was that Max was very passive. Even when he wanted something, he would just wait until someone gave it to him. His early intervention team mentioned to Lou and Elaine that they thought that his lack of initiation skills was a central concern. They explained that they wanted to be sure that Max developed skills in communicating independently—in making his wants known even when others could not guess them.

Initially, they started with manding (requesting) sessions. Max was shown a variety of his favorite treats, and the teacher would simply entice him with them. She might start to eat them herself, or she might say, "I have cheese doodles, I have carrots, and I have raisins," while showing them to Max. She did not make any other demands of Max.

As soon as Max indicated a desire, she gave him that item. At first, she gave him the treat whenever he just grabbed for it. Later, she required that he point to it, and later that he point and vocalize.

The teachers kept track of how often Max manded for things, and of how often he did it independently vs. with help from a teacher. They showed Lou and Elaine the charts, and they could see that Max was indeed asking for things, and doing it by himself!

Max continued to need a lot of training in manding over several years of home programming. He worked on manding for a variety of objects, using a full sentence, varying how he requested things, and requesting objects needed to complete or start an activity. In preschool, the emphasis continued, with targeted skills of manding from a peer and manding for information. Overall, his parents came to see Max's ability to mand as one of the most important survival skills with which they could equip him. Now, at age 6, he no longer required an adult to anticipate his needs or to indicate to him that he could request something he needed. They breathed a sigh of relief as they envisioned him in a setting with fewer supports; they knew he would make his desires and needs known!

Of course, manding was just one of many skills that Max needed to learn. Other deficits were also very important to address. One of the most significant was imitation. Unlike his brother, Max never imitated things he had seen others do. While his brother, Benjamin, had pretended to shave and mow the lawn like his Daddy while still a toddler, Max never did anything in that realm when he was a preschooler. The educational team emphasized to his parents that teaching Max to imitate was very important. Ultimately, if Max could learn to watch and do what others did, he could learn to play and to follow along with a group. These were critical skills for success in school.

Other skills Max needed to work on included labeling common objects, having conversational exchanges with others, playing appropriately with toys, following directions, and greeting others.

Lou and Elaine had decided on an intensive ABA model, and were scheduled for an observation at a center they had heard a great deal about. They were excited about the prospect of Max attending a school, but anxious about him being ready for school. They were also eager to learn more about how the center would teach Max, and they very much wanted to be part of the teaching team.

The Horowitz Family Learns about Programming

During a tour of an intensive behavioral preschool, Lou and Elaine had the opportunity to look at the instructional materials used by that center. There was a multi-page listing of the many potential goals a teacher might select for students in her class, and a series of notebooks crammed full of specific programs with details about how to teach the skills listed on the master curriculum. The program sheets looked confusing at first glance, but it became evident that they were a vital component of the center's program. Each sheet provided a systematic description of how to teach a particular skill. The director told Lou and Elaine that the teachers drew on these materials in setting up each child's instructional plans, but it was often necessary to modify the programs to meet the needs of an individual child. It was not just a matter of turning to the right page and following the directions in a cookbook fashion. Frequently the teacher had to try a program, modify it according to a child's preferences, strengths, and learning style, and then implement it.

The program sheets included a number of technical terms such as "Sd," "prompt," and "reinforcement," and the graphs included frequency, rate, goal lines, and notes. Lou and Elaine knew these terms were the jargon of applied behavior analysis. The director assured them that part of the training process for new parents was helping them understand this terminology so that they could support and be part of the learning that went on in the school. The words might sound technical, but they really were not so mysterious. It would not take long to understand this vocabulary well enough to read a sheet, implement a program, or interpret their child's performance from a graph.

What Does the Horowitz Family's Experience Mean for You?

A quality program for the education of children with autism will have a complete curriculum to draw upon for instructional purposes. This curriculum is 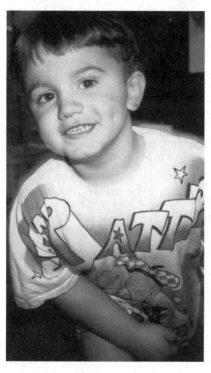 a road map that guides teachers in moving from one goal to the next. The curriculum must be comprehensive, addressing all of the deficits associated with autism. It must also be flexible, in that the specific programs being used must be modified according to a child's strengths and *learning style*— that is, according to the ways he processes information best. Some children may benefit more from visual input, others from auditory input or from using a motor skill such as tracing letters with a finger while naming them. Because there are so many individual differences among children, it is important that the curriculum be adaptable to the style of every child.

Lou and Elaine may have been a bit intimidated by the technical vocabulary they saw on the program sheets, but most parents are able to master this terminology without too much difficulty. Once you know the basics of behavioral language, you will be able to read and understand many of the instructional materials used in any teaching program. However, the behavioral skills involved in actually implementing these procedures require supervised experience to do well. Both parents and teachers alike should be well trained before they undertake this highly sophisticated instruction. That training must include extensive hands-on, supervised work. It is not sufficient to read about how to teach or to attend seminars. What is required to be competent is modeling by skilled teachers, rehearsal, and feedback.

Although the specific details of a curriculum will vary somewhat from one setting to another, the broad outlines will doubtless look similar. There will be programs to teach a child to request desired items, to label common objects, to follow instructions, to imitate what an adult or another child does, to use speech in functional ways, to play with toys, to play with another person, and so forth. Most preschool curricula respect the developmental nature of how children learn, and arrange these skills in a sequence that respects how one skill builds on another. For example, a child will be asked to imitate sounds before imitating words, or to match identical items before recognizing ones that are different. Some centers have or use a better-developed and more nuanced curriculum than others. This variation in quality is especially likely to be apparent when it comes to teaching advanced skills for language and socialization.

Programs also vary in the specific strategies that are used to teach a skill. In schools where staff members are more sophisticated in the use of applied behavior analysis, teachers are likely to apply behavioral methods with greater elegance than in those where staff members have only a passing familiarity with this technology. However, even very good teachers will differ in some of their teaching methods because not every aspect of applied behavior analysis has been objectively studied, and because children differ in their response to instructional strategies. For example, some teachers use "behavior specific praise" and some do not. That is, some teachers will name the behavior just completed by the child (e.g., "Good clapping"), while others will use more general praise (e.g., "Great work"). Teachers offer rationales for each strategy, and often match their praise statements to a student based on what type of praise he or she responds best to.

In this chapter, we will move from discussing the broad details of curriculum to describing the specific details of one little boy's instructional programs. Although there will not be enough detail to equip you to create programs for your child, this material will help you understand what goes into creating a curriculum.

A Sample Preschool Curriculum

The material in this chapter is based on the curriculum used in the School Program, our on-campus school for children with autism at Rutgers, the State University of New Jersey, as well as several commercially available curricula (e.g., Leaf & McEachin, 1999; Maurice, Green, & Luce, 1996; Sundberg & Partington, 1998; Taylor & McDonough, 1996). For more than 30 years, the Douglass Developmental Disabilities Center (DDDC) staff at Rutgers have been refining and developing our instructional material. Countless teachers and supervisors have contributed to its development and the material is part of a shared pool of information. It is not possible to give credit to any one person for a specific program because we have built one upon the other for a third of a century. The samples in this chapter reflect our collective creative effort.

Similar work has been going on in other centers and schools, and some of our teaching programs are undoubtedly similar to those in other programs around the world. This similarity arises because: 1) there are a number of tasks that are recognized as essential for children to learn; and 2) because behavioral teaching strategies are used in similar ways. Furthermore, you can utilize several curricular resources. At our center, we draw extensively on the ABLLS (Assessment of Basic Language and Learning Skills; Sundberg & Partington, 1998), especially for assessment and intervention in language areas, and we consult other resources for other areas as needed (Leaf & McEachin, 1999; Maurice, Green, & Luce, 1996; Sundberg & Partington, 1998; Taylor & McDonough, 1996).

A good curriculum should be a highly detailed itinerary describing the many, many skills that a child needs to master during the process of growing up. These skills should be organized in a logical fashion, and broken into small enough units that the child does not

have to take any "giant steps" from one item to the next. However, even the best curriculum has its limits. One of the things a curriculum does not tell us is how long it will take a child to learn a skill. Nor does a good curriculum ensure that a child will, in fact, learn all of the skills we would like him to master. Some children will progress slowly from item to item and may not be able to master every goal. Other children will move rapidly through instructional programs and at times will take leaps that allow them to move quickly from basic material to more advanced tasks. A child's progress may also be uneven from area to area. He may do quite well with gross motor skills and have more difficulties with language or socialization tasks. It is therefore important that each child be provided with an individualized instructional program that matches his own pace.

As the first step in developing an individualized program, the teacher will begin by assessing the child's current skills in each of the general areas on the curriculum. For example, she will explore the child's abilities in expressive and receptive language, social skills, and self-help activities. She will present tasks from various levels in each category and observe how the child performs on them. The child's checklist of skills is maintained over the years to show how he has progressed.

Some parents express concern about the "level" of programming at the beginning of intervention. It is not uncommon to feel that the first programs being taught involve basic skills that your child can already demonstrate. These foundation skills, however, are critically important, and your educational team may be ensuring that your child has strong skills to build upon. For example, it is essential that the child *consistently* demonstrate these skills. It is not enough for him to demonstrate a behavior "when he feels like it," or only occasionally. We need to be able to rely on these behaviors in order to build more complex skills.

It is not feasible to include here all of the instructional material from any domain of the curriculum we use at the Douglass Center. What follows are samples to give you a sense of how this material is organized. It would take a book or two to describe all of the many programs that comprise the total curriculum.

The Organization of a Curriculum

The components of a curriculum can be broken into broad categories including gross motor, fine motor, expressive language, receptive language, self-help, social skills, and academic/cognitive skills (Table 5-1). As shown in Table 5-2, these general categories can themselves be subdivided into finer units. For example, under the heading of expressive language are such specific skills as requesting and labeling and more advanced skills such as answering questions and having conversational exchanges. Self-help skills progress from the basics of feeding, dressing, and washing to more complex ones such as simple meal preparation, taking a shower, and selecting clothing for the day.

Table 5-1 | Some Broad Areas of Curricular Development

◆ Attending Skills	◆ Imitation
◆ Expressive Language	◆ Receptive Language
◆ Concept Formation	◆ Fine Motor
◆ Gross Motor	◆ Self-Help Skills
◆ Play Skills	◆ Social Skills
◆ School-relevant Skills	◆ Pre-Academic and Academic Skills

> **Table 5-2** | Examples of Sub-Headings under Expressive Language
>
> ◆ Requesting (Manding)
> ◆ Labelling
> ◆ Conversational Skills (Intraverbals)

Building Rapport and Interest in Instruction

Historically, we focused on compliance as a major issue for most children with autism. Many children respond to nearly any adult request with instantaneous resistance and attempts to escape from the demand. Most children with autism need to build a capacity for tolerance of teacher-led activities. In the past, ABA addressed compliance training, in part, by continuing with demands despite a child's protests. Instructors would simply persist, often prompting the child to do the target response when he would not do so independently.

In recent years, ABA interventionists have emphasized the use of reinforcement in building compliance. While this was always part of the means of building cooperation, it is now much more prominent. Teachers focus on making learning as reinforcing as possible, and on building the child's approach behaviors (e.g., the child repeatedly coming to the teacher and choosing to be with the teacher).

In the early stages of instruction, the instructor pairs him- or herself with highly rewarding activities, and slowly begins to introduce demands. Essentially, the instructor becomes an agent of reinforcement, and is associated with fun, with access to preferred items, and with reinforcement. Activities are initially child-led and child directed, in an effort to make the interaction as reinforcing as possible. For example, if the child likes bubbles, the instructor might make bubbles available, allowing the child to enjoy the preferred activity. Eventually, we make the transition into request training, so that the child begins to ask for bubbles. (See below.)

If a child frequently and intensely resists instruction, and pairing with reinforcers alone is not sufficiently building the child's interest and stamina for the learning situation, there may be a need to gradually help the child tolerate the teaching context itself. If so, the instructor may slowly increase the amount of time the child spends in a teaching interaction. First it may be one second, then two seconds, three seconds, five seconds, and so forth. Favorite toys may be made available to the child during instruction to increase the reinforcing power of sitting there. Gradually, other instructional demands will be paired with sitting.

Manding/Requesting Skills

One of the most significant deficits for children on the autism spectrum is in the area of manding (requesting). Even when students get good at labeling things and answering questions, they often fail to make their own needs known. This difficulty in spontaneous requesting has far-reaching implications, especially when students are in more inclusive classrooms where teachers cannot anticipate their needs. Manding should continue to be a focus of instruction, to ensure a well-developed capacity to communicate needs and desires and to ensure spontaneous communication.

Sample goals for manding include:

- Requesting via one word
- Requesting via 2 words
- Requesting using a sentence
- Requesting with eye contact
- Requesting using additional descriptors
- Requesting missing items needed for a task
- Requesting information

More information on teaching manding is available in *Incentives for Change: Motivating People with Autism Spectrum Disorders to Learn and Gain Independence* (Delmolino and Harris, 2004).

As mentioned at the beginning of this chapter, Max had tremendous difficulty asking for things he wanted. Even after he could label cookies and water and olives, he never requested them. His parents were puzzled. He might just watch the bowl of olives at a party or wait to be asked if he wanted water. It just didn't seem to occur to him that he could get desired items by asking for them!

Max needed lots of training in manding. At first, his teachers at home (and later at school) held manding sessions with him. In a manding session, they simply made available to Max things he really liked. They put them out, enticed him as best they could, and waited for him to indicate his desires. At first, he simply looked at the thing he wanted. Then he began reaching for items. Eventually, he started vocalizing for the things he wanted. The teachers were careful to make sure that the manding sessions were fun for Max.

Manding continued to be a focus for Max, even after he was requesting what he wanted. He still needed help learning all the different ways he could make requests. His teachers initiated programs to teach him to request an object when it was missing from a task (e.g., a puzzle piece), so that he could complete an activity. They also taught him to request items to begin an activity (e.g., a pair of scissors for an art project). In addition, they taught him to ask for information (such as where a treat was hidden or when a visitor would arrive). They made sure to generalize these skills to peers, so that Max understood that other children could be sources of help and information as well.

Imitation

One of the most salient difficulties of children with autism is their lack of imitative skills. They do not watch and do what those around them are doing. This deficit may be an early reflection of the same problems that result in difficulties with play and social skills. It is therefore critical for early intervention treatment plans to place a primary emphasis on imitation.

Teaching children to watch others and do as they do helps them learn to use objects and toys for functional purposes, to imitate facial movements needed to make certain sounds, and to follow along with a group. Both imitating body movements such as stamping feet or touching the head, and imitating use of objects such as stacking blocks or rolling a car, need to be taught specifically and systematically. Sample hierarchies for teaching in these areas are listed in Table 5-3. Instructions begin with very concrete one-step actions such as touching one's head or clapping. Because the focus is on imitation, not language comprehension, the instruction to imitate clapping would not be "Clap your hands." Rather, the adult would say "Do this," "Copy me," or "Do as I do," and clap her hands. As the child develops skills in simple imitation, two- and three-step imitation is taught. It is important to remember that the specific actions are not as important as the process of learning to watch and follow what other people do.

One of the happiest days in Lou and Elaine's life was when Max started copying them in their everyday chores. He imitated his Dad shaving and his Mom mowing the lawn. They didn't ask him to; he just did it! When they told his teacher, she said, "Yes, that's generalized imitation. That's what we've been waiting for."

Table 5-3 | Imitation Skills

General Progression of Motor Imitation

One-Step Commands
- A. Gross motor in chair (e.g., clap, arms up, stamp feet)
- B. Gross motor out of chair (e.g., jump, turn around)
- C. Fine motor (e.g., make a fist, point, thumbs up)
- D. Facial (e.g., stick out tongue, blow kiss)

Two-Step Commands
- A. Related (e.g., stand up and jump)
- B. Unrelated (e.g., clap and touch nose)

Three-Step Commands

Peer Imitation (imitating a child rather than an adult)

Generalization/Extensions of Imitation
- A. Actions to songs (e.g., "The Wheels on the Bus")
- B. Obstacle course (e.g., climbing over, around & under obstacles with another child)
- C. Observational learning (learning in group from other children)
- D. Imitation games (e.g., "Simon Says")

Table 5-4 | Imitation with Objects

General Progression of Imitation of Object Manipulation

One-Step Imitation
 A. Simple discrete actions (e.g., block in bucket, ring on stacker)
 B. Complex discrete actions (e.g., roll car on table, put bottle to baby's mouth)

Two-Step Imitation
 A. Related (e.g., put man in car & roll car, put baby in cradle & rock)
 B. Unrelated (e.g., put block in bucket & ring on stacker, put man in car & peg in pegboard)

Three-Step Imitation
 Related sequence at theme-based activity centers (e.g., farm toy, dollhouse, or amusement park toy)

Generalizations/Extensions of Imitation
 A. Pretend play with props (e.g., dress-up clothing, play kitchen)
 B. Task completion (finishing activity with toy)
 C. Peer imitation (playing with toys as peers do)
 D. Observational learning (learning to use toys or play games by watching peers)
 E. Play Stations (following peer actions at a sequence of stations.)

Expressive Language. Expressive language refers to the ability to communicate using speech or an alternative mode of communication. It includes many different functions of expressive communication, including requesting, labeling, and having a conversation. In Table 5-6, a parallel set of goals for expressive language is listed. Again, these might begin with early skills such as requesting by babbling for a child who makes no sounds, progress to requesting with verbal imitation, and advance to requesting objects by name. Other examples of expressive language goals include naming objects, naming actions, and answering the "Wh" questions (who, what, when, why).

The ability to vocally imitate is an important corollary skill to the development of vocal expressive language. However, expressive

Table 5-5 | Sample Receptive Language Skills

- Points to desired object
- Follows one-step command to "give"
- Follows one-step and two-step directions
- Points to body parts on self
- Discriminates actions in pictures
- Demonstrates functional use of objects
- Points to self and others in a group photo
- Knows concept of big and little using objects and pictures
- Identifies known community helpers
- Demonstrates comprehension of basic prepositions in relation to self, others, objects, and pictures
- Demonstrates receptive understanding of categories
- Identifies emotions in self and others

Table 5-6 | Sample Expressive Language Skills

- Requests desired items with gesture, picture, or word
- Requests desired items using full sentence (via sign, vocal language, or PECS)
- Requests missing items for task or activity
- Requests information
- Requests help
- Labels common objects
- Labels common actions
- Labels body parts
- Labels categories
- Answers social questions
- Answers "what" questions regarding picture
- Answers "where" questions regarding here and now
- Engages in reciprocal conversational exchanges

language is an important and achievable skill even for pre-vocal and nonvocal learners. You may wish to refer to the book *Meaningful Exchanges for People with Autism: An Introduction to Augmentative & Alternative Communication* by Joanne Cafiero (Woodbine House, 2005) for more information on nonverbal communication options for children with autism.

Language got off to a slow start, but then Max really took off. He did well receptively, but early expressive skills were tougher. He needed some intensive work in oral motor imitation and in verbal imitation to begin to make words that were understandable. Working on verbal imitation continued to be important to build the precision of Max's articulation, even when he was speaking in sentences.

Social and Play Skills

Like language skills, social skills are an essential part of the curriculum for every child with an autism spectrum disorder. The Douglass Center curriculum is very detailed in this domain. (See Table 5-7.) Early social skills include such behaviors as looking at oneself in the mirror and playing peek-a-boo. This basic awareness of self and others then branches out into skills for solo play, play with an adult, play with a child, and play in a group. It also includes learning the many social behaviors important to school life such as sitting in a circle, following group directions, and learning to assert oneself in an appropriate fashion.

Max had some strengths in social skills. He had always been somewhat interested in his brother, and he had some good early play skills even as a toddler. He used objects functionally, and he could persist with play for a while. He was somewhat rigid in his play, however. For example, it was hard for him to share play materials, because he wanted to arrange them all in a particular way. The teachers had to build his tolerance for sharing space and materials, and for deviating from his preferred plan for play.

Table 5-7 | Sample Play and Social Skills

- Responds to name
- Responds to praise and rewards delivered by adults
- Returns greetings
- Engages in parallel play
- Shares play materials
- Joins in finger plays and action songs
- Takes turns in a simple game
- Requests to join ongoing activity
- Engages in pretend play with objects
- Engages in pretend play assuming roles
- Initiates greetings and farewells
- Compliments others' works

Instructional Programs

A curriculum that consisted solely of a well-developed list of instructional goals would be of some help in developing an educational plan for a child with autism. However, in order to be truly useful, these lists must be linked to specific teaching programs. An effective curriculum should not only suggest a sequence of skills, but also tell the teacher how to teach those skills. For example, if your child has learned how to answer "who" questions and is ready to move on to "what" questions, there should be a program describing how to accomplish the new goals. These detailed instructional programs are at the heart of a child's education.

Understanding the Program Form

At the Douglass Center we use a special form for each instructional program. (See Figure 5-1 on page 107.) This Program Form provides a standardized format, ensuring that all the information is provided in a consistent fashion. It is likely that any well-run center- or school-based ABA program for children with ASD will use a similar form, documenting exactly how teaching will progress. If you can understand one Program Form used at the center your child attends, you will be well on your way to being able to read others as well. Table 5-8 lists the technical terms used on the form we use at the Douglass Center and gives a brief definition of each.

Figure 5-2 on page 108 depicts an actual instructional program used for Max during his first year in home-based, one-to-one instruction. Max was having problems making some sounds and needed help in learning how to place his tongue and lips to better articulate these sounds. This program, from the speech portion of the curriculum, was intended to help Max learn to imitate facial expressions.

There is a great deal of information included on the Program Form if you know how to read it. As you look at Figure 5-2, notice that there is a brief description of the *Target Behavior* that is described as "Imitates facial expressions: Oral motor movements." (Again, the "target behavior" is the behavior we want the child to learn (or in the case of challenging behaviors, to unlearn).) This target is then translated into the *Behavioral Objective* of imitating "oral motor movements within 2-3 seconds of the Sd [Discriminative Stimulus] presentation."

The abbreviation Sd (pronounced S D) is used in a Program Form to refer to an instruction or other event that tells a child it is time to do something. Examples of an Sd would be "Give me the book" or "Point to blue." An Sd can sometimes be nonverbal. For example, we might teach a child to wave when he sees another person wave. In that case the Sd would be the waving gesture of

Table 5-8 | Program Form Terminology

Behavioral Objective: Defines in observable terms the behavior under study. For example, the goal of reducing noncompliance might be defined as "John will comply with any instruction within 3 to 5 seconds of the command."

Praise: May be given as behavior-specific praise, telling a child exactly what he did right. An example of behavior-specific praise would be, "I like the way you put your toys away."

Consequence: A consequence is what happens as a result of the child's responding or failing to respond to an instruction. One common consequence of a correct response is to reinforce (reward) the child. If a child fails to respond or makes a mistake, the consequence may be a *correction* to guide a correct response.

Criterion: We need to decide when we will agree that a child has mastered a skill. Typically this calls for between 80% and 90% correct performance over two sessions or days. However, the criterion can be set at any level and is individualized to the child.

Data: Decision making in applied behavior analysis depends on the child's performance on a task. In order to evaluate progress, we collect data. That is, we make a record of how often the child is correct and how often he makes mistakes. There are many different ways to collect data, but all decisions about programming are based on data.

Probe: A probe is a procedure used to collect a sample of a child's progress in a teaching program. For example, a teacher might collect "probe data" by recording a child's response for the first trial of every teaching session.

Prompt: Help via a visual, verbal, or motor cue that indicates what a child should do. For vocal programs, this can range from a full prompt such as "Say 'duck'" to a partial prompt such as "d…" For a nonvocal response, a prompt may include hand over hand guidance, a model, a gesture such as pointing, or a cue within the object itself. Prompts are gradually faded as the child becomes more independent.

Sd: An Sd is a verbal instruction or other signal to a child that it is time to do a particular behavior. Examples of an Sd would be "do this" or "point to cow." If we teach a child to come to his mother when she calls his name, the calling of his name would be an Sd to go to his mother.

Target Behavior: A target behavior is the behavior being taught. Examples of target behaviors would be shoe tying, hand washing, or pointing to objects when named.

Figure 5-1

DOUGLASS SCHOOL
Educational Program Form

Student: **School Year:**

Area: **Coordinator:**

                                Date Initiated:

                                Date Mastered:

Target Behavior:

Behavioral Objective:

Description of Program:

Sd for Target Behavior:

Consequence:

Procedure:

Prompt Hierarchy:

Generalization:

Sets:

Materials:

Data:

Trials:

Criterion:

Program Comments:

Figure 5-2

DOUGLASS SCHOOL
Educational Program Form

Student: Max H.   **School Year:** 05-06

Area: Speech   **Coordinator:** Sally/Rae

Date Initiated: 9/20/05   **Date Mastered:** 2/05/06

Target Behavior: Imitates facial expressions: oral motor movements

Behavioral Objective: Max will imitate oral motor movements following a model within 2-3 seconds of Sd presentation

Description of Program: Establish sitting and attending behavior

Sd for Target Behavior:
"Do this"
"Copy me"
"Follow me"
"Do as I do"
"Watch and do"

Consequence: Reinforce correct responses with praise and tokens. If Max does not respond or responds incorrectly, provide appropriate correction.

Procedure:
Step 1: In a mirror side by side where Max can see your face and his own, present Sd. Physically prompt him through the movement using physical manipulation. Repeat the Sd. Max is prompted to repeat the action.
Step 2: In a mirror side by side where Max can see your face and his own, perform movement. Present Sd. Max is to imitate the action.

Figure 5-2 continued

Step 3: Siting face to face with Max, perform the movement. Present Sd. Max is to independently imitate without presence of the mirror.

Prompt Hierarchy:
  1. Full Physical Prompt (e.g., lightly press lips together)
  2. Partial Physical Prompt (e.g., lightly tap upper lip)
  3. Partial Visual Prompt (e.g., point to Max's lip)

Generalization: Mastery requires that you probe this skill varying the Sd, using at least two novel settings, sets of materials, and people. Criterion — 90% or above on at least two consecutive days.

Sets:
  1. lips together
  2. open mouth
  3. review Sets 1 & 2 mixed (Step 3 only)
  4. kissing
  5. bites lower lip
  6. review sets 4 & 5 mixed (Step 3 only)
  7. Places tongue between teeth

Materials: Mirror

Data: + = correct response, - = incorrect response, p = prompted response

Trials: up to 10 trials per day, separated in time, to ensure adequate practice

Criterion: 90% correct over two sessions

Program Comments:
  1. Use food as needed
  2. As Max masters each set in this program, related sets can be introduced in the imitation of words/syllables program. For example, mastery of Set 1 (lips together) would indicate introduction of words such as "me, bee, pie."

another person. In Max's program as shown in Figure 5-2, the Sd is both auditory ("Do this") and visual (the action is performed). That instruction is the signal to Max to respond by copying his teacher's behavior. Prior to being taught the relatively complex oral motor behaviors used in this program, Max had learned to imitate an adult on the command of "Do this" for simple behaviors such as clapping his hands or stamping his feet. Incidentally, there are many kinds of stimuli in applied behavior analysis (e.g., reinforcing and discriminative) and the *second letter always shows the type of stimulus*. For example, the symbol for a reinforcing stimulus is Sr.

In Max's program under the heading of *Description of Program,* the teacher is called upon to be certain she has Max's attention and that he is sitting quietly before she starts her instruction. However, not every applied behavior analyst requires these attending skills from the child before giving the instructions. Rather, they assume that as the child learns that following instructions brings rewards for responding correctly, the child will learn to attend and will not become dependent on an adult's instructions to do so. This is a good example of an area in which experts may differ. In practice, it is important to determine which approach is better for your child.

The learning we are asking Max to attempt is very demanding. We need to reward his efforts to help him stick to the task. Every instructional program therefore has a specified set of *Consequences.* In this case, the teacher is told to reinforce Max with praise and tokens. It is important that the praise statements chosen be meaningful and reinforcing to the child. The teacher might make a silly face that Max finds amusing or give him a hug, along with the praise statements. In that way she has praised his response, and then used that very behavior as an opportunity for a playful interaction.

If Max does not respond to the Sd or makes a mistake, the teacher has been instructed to "prompt" a correct response or to correct an error. In the early stages of learning, she would physically manipulate his face to help him shape his mouth or hold out an item such as a lollipop to encourage him to stick out his tongue. Later, she might use a subtler partial prompt such as tapping his lip very gently.

The next section of the program sheet describes the specific teaching *Procedure* in successive steps. In Step 1 the teacher or speech-language therapist sits next to Max and both face a mirror. First she gives the Sd "do this" and immediately she physically prompts Max to imitate. Then she repeats the command "do this," shows the model, but does not prompt and waits for Max to respond. She only prompts him if he does not comply after 2 seconds. In Step 2 the prompts are not routinely offered at the start of each trial and are reserved for trials in which Max does not obey the command. Finally, in Step 3 the mirror is removed and Max must respond when facing the therapist.

The *Prompt Hierarchy* describes the kinds of prompts to be used and the order of the prompts. In general, when teaching new skills, the teacher will use a "most to least" prompt hierarchy. This ensures that the student learns what is expected of him and makes the fewest errors possible. It also ensures that the student does not make repeated errors. Repeated errors can become error patterns that are difficult to reverse. In this progression, the teacher starts by giving a high level of assistance and ensuring a correct response, and then giving less assistance once the child begins to demonstrate some independence with the task. For example, the speech-language therapist is told to initially use a full prompt in which she helps Max press his lips together. Later she is to tap his lip, and eventually, if necessary, to point to his lip. Because children with ASD can become quite dependent on prompts, this guidance is always to be decreased in intensity as quickly as possible and used no more than essential.

Children with autism have problems transferring (generalizing) their skills from one setting to the next. As a result, it is important to plan for *Generalization* when writing their teaching programs. For example, Max must learn to imitate not only the specific behaviors that are being taught in the program, but new ones as well. We might test for this kind of generalization by modeling putting our tongue on our upper lip (a behavior he has not been taught) and seeing if he could imitate that new behavior. If he did, we would have evidence that he was able to generalize his imitative responses to new but similar behaviors. If he did not, we would teach more behaviors and then test again for generalization.

Generalization should also extend to other teachers and other settings. For example, in order to demonstrate that he can imitate the oral motor movements of a variety of people, Max would be expected to imitate his teacher and his mother as well as the speech-language therapist who initially trained him. For generalization to new places, he would be expected to follow the direction "do this" (or a synonymous instruction) when it was given at home as well as at school. Notice that according to the Program Form we have applied a 90% correct criterion to Max's performance in the generalization portion of the program. He must get 9 out of 10 opportunities correct for three days in a row on the generalization tasks before it is considered adequately generalized.

Another important form of generalization is across instructions. That is, a child should learn to follow different commands that mean the same thing. For example, "Follow me," "Do this," "Copy me," and "Do what I do." These instructions are all variations on the same theme and a child may encounter different wordings in his natural environment. We try to accomplish this type of generalization from the beginning of a program, using varied and naturalistic instructions. Occasionally, a student may require a more systematic broadening of instructions. In these cases, we may begin with one simple phrase, and then quickly expand.

The *Sets* section of the program lists the specific skills Max is to master. This includes pressing his lips together, opening his mouth, and so forth. Notice that the first few items are the ones that are most easily prompted with physical guidance, while the later items, such as placing tongue between teeth, are harder to prompt. We expect that as Max learns to imitate oral movements he will need fewer and fewer prompts for each new movement. Notice also that Max is being taught to discriminate among the different items by mixing two or more items, one of which he already knows, in the same session. He must put his lips together when that is the model and open his mouth when that task is requested. In order to do this, Max must learn to attend carefully to the teacher's behavior.

In this particular program we did not specify any particular *Materials* except the mirror. For some programs, we might list items to be used in teaching, such as blocks, trucks, dolls, and so forth.

In the *Data* section, the therapist has been asked to record Max's performance using a "+" to signify that he was correct and a "-" when he was incorrect. Sometimes she might also be told to record a "p" to indicate he was prompted on a trial.

At the bottom of the Program Form under *Trials* is information indicating that the therapist should do 10 to 20 trials a day, and that according to the *Criterion* section Max must respond at 90 percent correct over two sessions in a row before he moves to the next set of tasks. (Note: even if a child is doing 10 or more trials per day of a program, we would not do all of those trials in a row or in one sitting.)

Finally, under *Program Comments,* the speech therapist is told that she should use food as necessary to motivate Max and that as he masters the oral motor skills they should be incorporated into his other speech programs.

Programs Mastered Over One Year

Max worked on many instructional programs related to speech and language over the course of one year. Table 5-9 shows a partial list of speech and language programs he mastered during the year.

Along with his instruction in speech and language, Max also benefited from similarly detailed programs in the domains of social skills. See Table 5-10 for a list of the social and play programs he learned in a year. Inspecting the sample programs for social skills in Figures 5-3 (pages 116-117) and 5-4 (pages 118-119) may

---

Table 5-9 | Speech and Language Programs Mastered by Max in One Year at School

- Follows commands with two steps or involving two objects
- Names object based on verbal information
- Uses subject pronouns (I, you, he, she, and it)
- Correctly responds to "what" questions regarding common objects and events
- Correctly responds to "what" questions: Describes use of senses
- Correctly responds to "when" questions
- Discriminates among who, what, where questions
- Understands and uses prepositions
- Labels attributes of objects
- Uses adjective-noun combinations appropriately
- Names sensations
- Labels emotions in self, others, and stories
- Answers specific questions about activity just completed
- Uses irregular past tense verbs
- Tells a story with props
- Requests desired items spontaneously
- Requests information needed to find objects
- Requests help
- Engages in topical reciprocal conversation up to 6 exchanges
- Can describe similarities and differences (people, objects)
- Says "I don't know" appropriately

Table 5-10 | Some of the Social and Play Skills
Mastered by Max in One Year at School

- Initiates social contact with an adult ("Look at this," "Play with me")
- Initiates social contact with peers (e.g., asks another child, "Can I play with you?")
- Plays appropriately (parallel) in a group of other children for up to 10 minutes
- Cooperates in simple games with adult or child for up to 10 minutes
- Interacts reciprocally in a group of children (5 exchanges)
- Assumes a character role in pretend play activity (e.g., police officer, teacher, daddy)
- Acts out a familiar routine with peer for up to 5 minutes (e.g., going shopping)
- Invites another child to play a specific game
- Chooses the correct emotional response for a given real situation
- Answers questions from a peer
- Spontaneously imitates actions of peers
- Offers assistance to peers

give you an idea of the complexity of creating a full curriculum for a child with autism. Even if the teacher works in a setting that has a fully developed curriculum, she must be able to select those programs that are suitable for a child and adapt them to the child's specific leaning style.

Although some of the early programming for items like noun labels or pointing to a color may seem relatively straightforward, the demands on teacher and child grow increasingly more complex. A good example of a more complex social skill is complimenting another child. Among the precursors to learning when and how to say nice things to someone else are: a) social initiations, b) adequate speech, c) understanding the context for giving others compliments, d) reciprocal conversation, e) respecting physical space, and so forth. Each of these skills in turn has its own precursors! It is this complexity that makes a skilled teacher or consultant so vital.

Figure 5-3

DOUGLASS SCHOOL
Educational Program Form

Student: Max   **School Year:** 05-06

Area: Social Skills   **Coordinator:** Bob

Date Initiated: 10/26/05   **Date Mastered:** 1/8/06

Target Behavior: Keeping appropriate distance from other child

Behavioral Objective: Max will select a bubble to stand in that is an appropriate distance from a peer. He will stand in space while speaking to peer.

Description of Program: Establish group attention

Sd for Target Behavior:
"Show me where you stand when you talk to a friend."
"Find a spot to talk to your friends."
"Talk to a friend."

Consequence: Each child will receive a token for standing in the circle the whole time

Procedure: *(Presented via rule card and then rehearsed)*
  1. Discuss rules for standing near a friend.
  2. Select one child to stand in a circle.
  3. Select another child to pick the circle they would stand in if they wanted to talk to that friend.
  4. Once in the appropriate circle, the second child expresses (reiterates) the rules: I'm not too close, I'm not too far, if I could reach my arms out straight, I'd touch my friend's shoulders.
  5. After saying the rules, the children say "hi" to each other.

Prompt Hierarchy: Initially Max should not be in first three couplets. Gradually move him forward until he goes first. Whisper rules as needed.

Figure 5-3 continued

> **Generalization:** Ensure that Max can play game with every other child in class.
>
> **Sets:** Not applicable.
>
> **Materials:** Bubble markers on floor (to be faded before mastery).
>
> **Data:** + = correct, - = incorrect. Collect as probe data.
>
> **Trials:** Max should have at least three turns each time game is played.
>
> **Criterion:** Selects correct bubble and repeats rules independently when playing game two days in succession.
>
> **Program Comments:** Entire preschool class plays game.

A Few Thorny Questions

Many parents share the same questions about applied behavior analysis when they are thinking about intensive behavioral intervention for their child. This section answers some questions that come up quite frequently.

Why Are Reinforcers Important?

The role of reinforcement is to increase the likelihood that a child will repeat a desired response under similar conditions in the future. The verbal feedback that accompanies a tangible reward is one way of informing the child that he or she has made the correct response. However, for many children with autism, that feedback is not salient enough to produce changes in future responses. We need to add more concrete feedback in the form of tangible rewards. Without such rewards, learning would be nearly impossible.

Figure 5-4

DOUGLASS SCHOOL
Educational Program Form

Student: Max   **School Year:** 05-06

Area: Social Skills   **Coordinator:** Emmet

Date Initiated: 2/06   **Date Mastered:** 6/06

Target Behavior: Engage in conversation with peers.

Behavioral Objective: Max, standing in circle of peers, will select a conversational card and have at least one thing to say about that topic. He will attend while others speak.

Description of Program: Establish group attention. At least 4 children in circle including Max.

Sd for Target Behavior:
"It is conversation time. Max, please come up and choose a topic."
"Let's chat. Who would like to pick a topic?"
"Time to talk with friends. Let's check the board to see who our talking leader is today."

Consequence: Behavior specific praise.

Procedure:
1. Have each child stand in conversational circle.
2. Place the interest cards around the circle.
3. Explain the rules of the game on the rule card. Tell the children they can take turns choosing an interest card. One child chooses a card and places it in their circle. When the card is in their circle that is the topic of conversation. Everyone in the conversation circle must talk about that topic. When the conversation is over or everyone has talked on the topic (encourage it to go as naturally as possible), the next child can pick an interest card.

Figure 5-4 continued

> **Prompt Hierarchy:** Initially Max should not be among first
> three children to take a turn choosing card. Gradually move him
> forward in the sequence. Whisper rules as needed.
>
> **Generalization:** Max should be able to play Conversation
> Circle with any randomly selected group of 4 children in class.
>
> **Sets:** Not applicable.
>
> **Materials:**
>   1. Masking tape to make circles on floor large enough for each
>   child in group. Circles should be large enough for each child
>   to stand in and locate appropriate distance from other circles.
>   2. 5 to 10 interest cards. Sports, seasons, holidays, superheroes,
> etc. Build up to 20 interest cards, then randomize.
>
> **Data:** + = correct, - = incorrect, p= prompted. Collect as
> probe data.
>
> **Trials:** Each child including Max should have at least 3
> opportunities in a game.
>
> **Criterion:** Follows all rules correctly without prompts on six
> successive days across six different topics.
>
> **Program Comments:** At least four children in group. Rotate
> group members. Vary the cards to ensure continuing interest.

Because children with autism may not care about pleasing us
and because the learning required of them is so demanding, it is
important to offer them highly desirable rewards. Although reinforcements (rewards) can include tangible things like food, tickles,
and hugs, good teachers always combine these items with verbal
praise. When words of approval are paired repeatedly with more
tangible rewards, the words gradually become very powerful by
themselves. However, for many small children in the early stages
of learning, food may be the only powerful reinforcement available.
The treat is divided into tiny portions so that the child does not get

his fill too quickly and we vary the foods. We also use lavish praise that will gradually become rewarding for most children because it has been paired with the food.

Some parents ask whether a child will gain weight under this approach. We have never seen it happen. The food is offered in tiny bites. In addition, contrary to the stereotype, we rarely use chocolate candies as a reward. Tastes of yogurt, pickles, olives, pretzels, and little chunks of apple are typical food rewards. Of course, each child's rewards must fit his preferences. If the food is not attractive, it will not be a reinforcement for the child and learning will not go well.

Tangible rewards such as food are gradually faded (phased out) over time so the child will not become dependent on them and will not expect them after each trial. For example, after some months of teaching, the only food reward might be a snack at the end of a full lesson.

What Does It Mean If a Child Does Not Make Progress?

Sometimes children fail to make rapid progress on an ABA program. There can be several reasons for this. One is that the child is not motivated to do the work. In that case, it is important to consider using more powerful rewards. Another possibility is that the child has been asked to make too great a leap in learning. We may have left out some important intermediate skills. For example, if we are trying to teach a child to initiate a play interaction with another child, we would need to ensure that he knew how to play the game, knew how to say the words, and had an appropriate way of approaching the other child. Without the prerequisite skills, the child may not be able to fill in the gaps on his own. Sometimes we may have chosen the wrong learning modality for helping a child learn a task. For example, if the child is more of a visual than an auditory learner, we may need to offer visual cues such as pictures to help him with a lesson.

For a small minority of children with ASD, learning is limited by severe mental retardation, childhood disintegrative disorder, or Rett's disorder. Although all children with autism can learn compliance, imitation, functional communication, and adaptive skills such as dressing, hygiene, or household routines, some children may not be able to master higher-order social skills or vocal expressive language. These children may find the sheer intensity of the methods we have described to be very stressful because of their limited ability to master new skills. For these children, we make modifications in the teaching approach. For example, modifications might include a more visually based curriculum, fewer language demands, a greater emphasis on self-help and daily living skills, and more frequent rewards.

Often it takes a skilled behavior analyst to determine why a child is not learning a lesson. Parents may develop that level of skill eventually, but it is a sophisticated assessment process that requires expertise.

What If My Child Won't Cooperate?

Noncompliance (uncooperative behavior) is often a problem in the early stages of teaching. As discussed earlier in this chapter, it is important that we instructors pair ourselves with access to reinforcement, and build approach behaviors in the children with whom we work.

When noncompliance occurs later in teaching, it may signal the need for an adjustment in the curriculum. Solving these problems is the role of your home consultant or your child's teacher. This kind of troubleshooting requires an intimate knowledge of a dynamic curriculum that can shift and change in response to the child's needs. Sometimes we may have made too great a leap for a child from one program to the next, and sometimes we may be asking a child to respond in a modality that is especially difficult for him. Some children require more novelty than others, and need the tasks to be varied on a continual basis.

How Does an ABA Curriculum Relate to the IFSP or IEP?

As Chapter 1 explains, children who receive any publicly funded early intervention or special education services in the U.S. are required to have an IFSP (if under the age of 3) or an IEP (if over the age of 3). These documents list the short-term objectives and long-term goals that have been developed for the child in each developmental area or academic subject in which he is experiencing difficulty. They also specify what services will be provided to help the child meet his goals and in what setting the services will be provided. The IEP and IFSP are frequently reviewed and modified to reflect the child's changing needs.

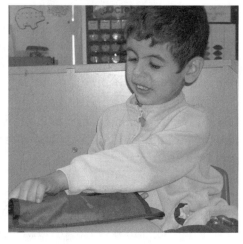

It should be easy to link your child's teaching programs to his IEP. Part of the strength of applied behavior analysis is that goals and objectives are specific and measurable. That kind of objectivity is also central to every IEP. In our work in helping our preschoolers make the transition to less restrictive settings, we often find that school personnel are receptive to incorporating our goals directly into the IEP. In some cases, they might instead attach our plan to the IEP document with a note to see the attachment.

When more than one agency is providing services to your child, it is crucial that everyone is "reading from the same page." Although following the IEP helps in that regard, the IEP document itself does not have enough detail to ensure that different people will do the same things. As a result, you as a parent or someone else involved in coordinating your child's education must ensure that everyone is using the same methods to reach goals. This collaborative approach is vital if your child is not to be confused and frustrated by having different people hold different expectations. At the Douglass Center, we invite parents, outside professionals including members of the child study team, and our own staff to come together to discuss plans and agree on joint strategies. We have found that when we fail to do this, it is the child who pays the price. If your child's program does not provide for these kinds of meetings you might ask staff to consider holding one. You may also invite the people who develop your child's ABA program to your child's IEP meeting with the school district.

In Sum

A comprehensive curriculum is a vital tool for any center-based, school-based, or home-based program. This curriculum is the roadmap that helps teachers plan a child's instructional programs and move from one goal to the next. Not only should there be a well-ordered sequence of goals, but also instructional programs to support each goal. In addition to having access to a good curriculum, it is essential that the teacher be sufficiently experienced to know when to deviate from the curriculum and how to adapt the teaching programs to each child's needs. The curriculum is a guide to help facilitate teaching. Each child, however, is unique and will have needs that must be met through a highly individualized program.

Parents Speak

Autism has put a hole in my heart that is hard to repair. To watch my son struggle with life's simplest tasks can be overwhelming at times. Thinking of him in therapy for hours instead of playing with his friends or going to a movie is torture for me. But I know it's what is best for him and it's what he needs right now. Because of all the progress he has made, it makes it a bit easier to take. Will he ever be like other little boys? I don't know. I do know that I love him just the way he is and that he has taught me to be excited by things we take for granted each day. Each milestone he reaches I will be by his side to applaud him. I do believe in miracles and yes, maybe someday, I will dance with him at his wedding.

෮෯

The school has been great about teaching us how to understand what they are doing for our son. The home support consultant comes to see us every couple of weeks. She brings programs and shows us how to use them. She always asks us what we want and works with us to write the programs to help with problems around the house. For example, we wanted to find some way for our two-year-old to start to play with Jack. The consultant gave us a program that they both love.

෮෯

The first time we visited the school, they showed us this thick book full of programs and charts and said they had one for each child. I was really impressed because all of the goals and everything was so clear.

෮෯

We did a home-based program for more than a year. Our consultant really knew what he was doing. He helped us plan step by step what to teach Sara. And he taught us the methods to use in teaching every program. What a blessing he was. We had to learn a lot, but we had a fabulous teacher.

෮෯

We chose the school because our research led us to believe that applied behavior analysis held the greatest hope for our son's progress. The school was the most rigorous in following ABA of all the schools we looked at. Some explained that they used a more "humane" approach, but we believed the most "humane" thing we could do for our son was to give him the best possible chance to progress. We liked the fact that the school is actively involved in research.

ᘒ

We were convinced early on that ABA offered the best-documented, broadest-based improvement for kids with autism. Other approaches were more "seductive," but we wanted to give our son the best possible long-range chance for a full life.

We've been lucky in that we never had a major problem with a professional who was working with our son, probably due in part to doing homework up front before selecting the therapists and the programs.

ᘒ

There is so much controversy over what to teach and when to teach it. It is a little dizzying. I know that for me the answers were in my son's progress. Was he getting better? Doing things he could not do before? More in tune with everyone and everything? Yes, Yes, Yes. I learned to value not just the numbers in a book, but what he did every day, with us and in the neighborhood. That's the change that really makes a difference. It always delighted me when people on the block commented on his progress. That's what it's all about!

Curricular References

Here are a couple of good guides to curricula for children with autism. By themselves, these guides will not enable you to educate a child, but used in conjunction with behavioral teaching skills they could be quite valuable in setting up and continually developing a teaching program. The references are based on years of work by multiple excellent clinicians in nationally recognized programs.

Leaf, R. & McEachin, J. (1999). *A work in progress: Behavior management strategies and a curriculum for intensive behavioral treatment of autism.* New York, NY: DRL Books.

Maurice, C., Green, G., & Luce, S. C. (1996). *Behavioral intervention for young children with autism: A guide for parents and professionals.* (See especially chapter by Taylor and McDonough.)

Partington, J. & Sundberg, M. (1998). *The Assessment of Basic Language and Learning Skills (ABLLS).* Pleasant Hill, CA: Behavior Analysts, Inc. (Assessment and Curricular Planning Tool)

Romanczyk, R. G., Lockshin, S., & Matey, L. (1997). *The individualized goal section curriculum – Version 9.0.* Apalachin, NY: CBTA.

Sundberg, M. L. & Partington, J. W. (1998). *Teaching language to children with autism or other developmental disabilities.* Pleasant Hill, CA: Behavior Analysts, Inc.

6 | Choosing a Program

The Mishra Family: Confusion about Intervention for Autism

Anita and Veer Mishra were very worried about their four-year-old son, Gopal. Until recently, Anita and Veer had attributed Gopal's delays to the use of two languages in the home. They were comforted by his clear intelligence. He already knew his letters and numbers, he could count, and he read simple words in books. On a family visit to India, however, he had spent a great deal of time with his cousins, and they saw how very isolated he appeared. He did not seek his cousins' company, and was quite content to quietly lie on the floor and move trains while he squinted his eyes.

When the Mishras returned to the U.S., they immediately saw their pediatrician, who recommended an evaluation by a specialist. When Gopal was diagnosed with PDD-NOS, they realized that he would not be ready to start preschool in the fall, as they'd planned. Instead, he would need specialized teaching to help him learn the social and communication skills that would hopefully enable him to attend the neighborhood school someday.... The search for an appropriate placement was overwhelming, and they realized that they needed to learn a great deal very rapidly. They heard different recommendations from different sources, and soon found their heads spinning.

Ultimately, they decided to seek an early intervention/preschool program that used applied behavior analysis, as it was the only option with data to support its effectiveness. As researchers by trade, Gopal's parents liked the idea of data being used to guide decisions, and were comfortable with the precise and accountable nature of the intervention.

Even after they made this choice, however, they continued to be confused. There was a tremendous amount of information available within ABA, but sometimes it was difficult to sort through it all. They also encountered a lot of opinions among professionals and other parents that were sometimes difficult to understand. For example, some people told them to avoid programs using Discrete Trial Instruction, or to consider only programs utilizing a Verbal Behavior approach (which actually refers to the use of a language classification system developed by B. F. Skinner). Others emphasized the need for Discrete Trial instruction, or recommended a "Lovaas" program. They read about Incidental Teaching, Natural Environment Training, and Pivotal Response Training, but had difficulty understanding how they all differed from one another and which were important for their son. Some people they spoke to alluded to "new ABA" and "old ABA", suggesting that some techniques or strategies may be outmoded and even harmful. The more they read and spoke to people, the more confused they became.

Ultimately, they decided to tour the ABA programs within about a 30 mile radius of their home and get a feel for the ways in which different programs approached teaching. As they toured the programs, they began to understand the differences between naturalistic ABA strategies and more formal ABA instructional approaches. They also attended some conferences and workshops on ABA intervention, and began to get their questions answered.

They followed the checklist offered by their local autism support organization in asking questions about each program. This checklist helped them identify other crucial aspects of the learning environment, including number of children in the class, ratio of children to adults in the setting, and the ability levels of the children in the classes targeted for Gopal.

Confusion about Intervention: Every Family's Story

How is Gopal's family experience similar to your own? Choosing an intervention for your child with an autism spectrum disorder is probably one of the most difficult and anxiety-provoking decisions you will ever face. What are the important qualities to look for in a potential program? What is important to understand about ABA?

It is very important to personally see the programs that may serve your child. A professional from your school district may make suggestions based on his or her experience in placing other children, and may wish to go with you on the visits. However, no amount of professional judgment can replace your own opinion as a parent. Professionals can be your consultants and members of your team, but they are not your bosses!

Anita and Veer visited each of the schools that had been suggested to them, and asked a series of questions to ensure they were satisfied with the resources that were available. They were always careful to be respectful of the program and not to appear critical in their evaluation, but they were relentless in asking for the information that would allow them to decide who could best serve Gopal. They found that program directors met their inquiries with varying openness, and that some appeared annoyed by the specifics of their questions. They were most comfortable with the programs where staff addressed their questions thoroughly, and felt that such openness and nondefensiveness was a good indicator of the kind of future parent-professional collaboration they were seeking.

In this chapter, we will first address some of the global indicators of a high quality program that you should keep in mind while you are doing your observations. We will then address the important elements of instruction in an ABA approach.

Choosing a Program: Global Indicators of Quality

The program you select for your child can have a far-reaching impact on her welfare. In the previous chapters of this book we have touched on a variety of features you might hope to find in an educational program for a child with autism. This chapter brings that information together in a fashion that is convenient for you.

> **Table 6-1** | Questions to Consider in
> Visiting a Program

The Children and the Services

- Who are the children in the program?
- What are the functioning levels of the children?
- Does the program offer the services your child needs?
- How many hours of instruction are offered?
- Is the program year-round?
- How does the program support transition to new services?

Meeting the Unique Needs of Each Child

- Does the program follow the children's IFSPs or IEPs?
- How is the child's progress evaluated?
- Is the ratio of adults to children correct for your child?

Home Support Services

- Will you be offered training in applied behavior analysis?
- Will staff members be available to help you develop home programs?
- Are parent and/or sibling support groups available?

Supervision and Accountability

- How are the staff members supervised?
- How do staff members stay up-to-date on teaching methods?
- Are there staff members who are board certified in behavior analysis?
- Are staff members and students "on-target" most of the time?
- Is it clear who is in charge of the program?

Use the items in Table 6-1 as an outline to follow in organizing the information you collect about the programs you visit.

The Children and the Services

Who Is Served?

Look for a classroom that is designed specifically for children with autism spectrum disorders. Some early intervention programs and preschool programs are called "generic," "mixed disability," or "preschool handicapped" programs because they serve children with a range of disabilities. You might find children with attention-deficit/hyperactivity disorder, mental retardation, language delay, and autism in a single preschool class. That kind of mix is not usually in the best interests of a young child with an autism spectrum disorder, who needs very special and intensive educational services. Because the educational needs of children with autism are so highly specialized, it is unusual to find those resources offered in a classroom that serves a blend of children with various diagnoses. Other children may not need the intensity, the precise structure, the great consistency, the flexibility, and the individualization in the use of applied behavior analysis that is so essential to children with autism.

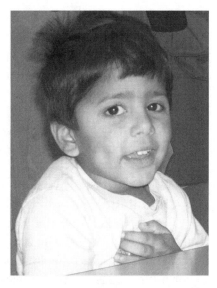

Although there may be exceptions, most "generic" special education preschool classes will not have the teaching technology and staffing resources required by the young child with autism. In our opinion, a good home-based program or a class in another school district that offers specialized services will almost invariably be better for a child with an autism spectrum disorder than a generic preschool class. In a cooperative school district, you may be able to work closely with your district to create an appropriate program for children with autism. In an uncooperative district, you may need to assert your legal rights to get the services your child needs.

What Is the Functioning Level of the Children?

Look for a classroom in which the children's abilities are roughly comparable to your child's abilities. There will certainly be variation among children, but you want your child to be with others whose needs are similar and who can provide appropriate stimulation. If your child's skills are markedly superior to those of every other child in the class, she might be a fine model for them, but she would probably lack models for herself. On the other hand, if your child's skills are markedly lower than the other children's skills, it may be difficult for her to comprehend group lessons or to be paired with a similarly skilled learner for small group instruction.

What Kind of Support Services Does Your Child Require?

Look for a classroom that has the specialized support services your child needs. The most important support services are a speech-language specialist to build language skills and a behavior analyst to consult on behavioral and learning issues. In addition, some children need other services such as physical therapy. Does the program offer those services? If not, can you arrange to have them provided before or after school in another setting? For example, at the Douglass Center we do not have physical therapy or occupational therapy. Parents who wish to obtain these services for their child schedule them after school. We have found school districts to be very cooperative in making these arrangements.

It is not unusual for a small program that specializes in treating children with autism not to have their own physical therapist or adaptive physical education specialist. However, if your child needs that service, or any other, you will want to be certain it is part of her educational plan.

How Many Hours of Instruction Will Your Child Receive?

Look for a program that offers five days a week of full-day instruction. Young children with autism need an intensive educational experience if they are to make optimal progress. A couple of hours a day, one or two days a week, will not do the job. As we explained in our discussion of the work of Ivar Lovaas in Chapter 2, those children in the 10-hour-a-week program did not make much progress, while nearly half of those in the 40-hour-a-week program did very well.

The program you are evaluating may not offer 40 hours a week of instruction, but they should be prepared to work with you to help you supplement that instruction to bring it up to 40 hours. At the Douglass Center we provide 25 hours a week of teaching in school and expect parents to supplement that with 15 hours a week at home. We give parents the written home programs and support they need to carry out that home instruction.

Is It a Year Round Program?

Look for a program that is open all year. Summer vacation is a lot of fun for typically developing children, but often a burden for children with autism spectrum disorders who struggle with un-structured time and may lose skills without practice. They cannot afford to take the summer "off." Children with autism seem to be especially vulnerable to losing hard-won ground over a prolonged summer break. Although most programs do close for vacation pe-riods, it is probably better to have these breaks scattered through the year and not taken in one long chunk over the summer.

What Happens When a Child Graduates from the Specialized Placement?

Quality programs always have specific procedures they use to follow up on a child's progress after she graduates from the services of that center. For example, at the Douglass Center, a member of our staff is available to visit the child in the new placement and to consult with the new teacher about programming concerns. We find that many schools are very receptive to this continuing consultation, while a few reject our offer of help. After the new placement has been identified, we visit with the parents and personnel from the school district, talk with the new teacher and invite him or her to come to our program, and collaborate with the future placement in making a gradual transition from one setting to the next. Typically, one of our staff members goes with the child during these transition visits. That allows us to support the child while she is adapting to the new class, and to teach her new skills that may be essential to the move.

It is important that you evaluate how the program plans for successful transitions to other settings. The results of teaching efforts can be severely damaged with a poorly planned transition process. Effectively planning for a good transition is a challenge for some school districts, whose personnel often do not begin to plan for September until August. When the time comes, you may have to advocate heavily with your district for appropriate and timely planning. At this stage, you can discuss how the preschool placement you are seeking will help in engineering that ultimate transition to kindergarten or first grade.

Meeting the Unique Needs of Your Child
Does the Program Follow a Child's Educational Plan?
Look for a program in which instruction is linked to the child's educational plan. Every child should have either an Individualized Family Service Plan (IFSP) or an Individualized Educational Program (IEP). The IFSP is used in early intervention programs for children under the age of 3 years, while the IEP is used for children enrolled in preschool or school-age programs.

In either case, this plan is the road map for your child's education. It describes the goals of the educational program and the means to be used to achieve those goals. These goals should be written in behavior-specific language that clearly defines the desired skills and allows skill acquisition to be measured. For example, the goal

"Relates to other children" is vague and hard to measure. If the IEP said, "Emma will approach another child and invite that child to play a game of catch" that would be specific and measurable. You have the right to be an active participant in the development of your child's plan, and should not accept a plan unless you agree with it.

To get a sense of how well staff at a program follows IEP's, ask staff how they ensure following each child's IEP. They may show you evidence of those efforts, which could include daily data sheets that list a child's IEP goals.

How Is a Child's Progress Evaluated?

Look for a program that keeps careful records on each child's progress. Data collected about a child's performance should be kept in an organized fashion. Often the data are recorded on a graph so that it is possible to track the child's progress visually.

In quality programs, data are not only kept, but used. Decisions about when to change programs and whether or not a child is making progress should always be based on data. You should not expect a program to show you an individual child's data, because of privacy issues. However, they may show you samples without any identifying information or they may share blank forms they use for recording data.

What Is the Staff Ratio?

Look for a program that has enough adults to meet the needs of your child. Most very young children with autism who are just starting an instructional program require a one-to-one ratio most of the time. Other children who have mastered some of the basic skills will be better off with somewhat less intense teaching because they need to learn how to share a teacher's attention, learn in a group, and do independent work. It is important that the classroom have enough well-trained staff to meet your child's needs.

Signs that there might not be enough staff in a program include seeing children left alone to amuse themselves for extended periods of time and children waiting prolonged periods for responses to their needs or requests.

Home Support Resources

Are Parents Offered Training in the Program's Teaching Methods?

A great deal of research documents that it is very important to the progress of the child with autism that parents support school's efforts. Consistency from one setting to another is essential in ensuring that your child makes the best progress possible. This consistency is important to helping her transfer newly learned skills from the school to other settings. This process of transfer is sometimes called "generalization," a term which can refer to the notion that skills learned in one setting with one teacher should be able to be used in many settings with many different people.

Research also shows that parents can master any of the teaching skills used in the classroom. The experience of parents who rely on home-based instruction demonstrates that parents can become highly skilled in the use of behavioral teaching methods. A quality program should offer you the opportunity to learn about the teaching methods that are employed in the school and help you reach a level of proficiency that will enable you to do home programming with your child.

You may then opt to do direct instruction with your child—for example, teaching her *new* skills and concepts that the program staff suggests you work on. Or, instead, you may opt to be a generalization agent, working on skills that have been *mastered* at school and ensuring that she demonstrates them with you at home too. Either way, be sure the program you select will support you in your efforts to instruct your child. While both types of instruction require training, in general you will need more training for teaching new skills. You will also want to be sure to be consistent with how you are teaching the skill between home and school, if the skill is a new or emerging one.

Are Staff Members Available to Visit Your Home on a Regular Basis?

Although some programs provide home programming for parents only at onsite at the center or school, many quality programs send a staff member to families' homes to consult. This consultation includes help in designing programs to address specific problems at home as well as help to ensure a smooth transfer of programs being done in the school to the home.

Does the Program Provide Parent and/or Sibling Support Groups?

Raising a child with autism is a very stressful experience that has an impact on parents and siblings alike. Family members are often called upon to sacrifice time, privacy, emotional energy, and control over their lives, which can result in significant stress. Parents have told us that no one understands that stress better than another parent who has been down the same road. Recognizing the existence of this stress and the potential benefits of mutual support, many quality programs offer parent support groups, and some also offer sibling support groups. These groups give members a safe place in which to reflect on the experience of living with a child with autism, share coping strategies, and offer one another the mutual respect and caring that makes it easier to manage in the face of stress.

Sibling services may include a support group that meets on a regular basis, a sibling visiting day, or an activity day for siblings. Any of these services allows siblings to meet other children in similar circumstances, reducing the isolation they may feel in their situation. It can also allow for education in autism, for explanations of how children with autism learn, and for training in skills that will make them more successful in their interactions with their sibling.

If the program in which your child is enrolled does not offer support groups or if you have a home-based program, you may want to consider seeking a group elsewhere. For example, some state chapters of the Autism Society of America provide this service to their members.

Supervision and Accountability

How Are Teachers Supervised?

No matter how experienced and skilled a teacher may be, it is valuable to have periodic supervision available. For younger, less experienced team members, this supervision is vital. The program should provide for the supervisor to periodically observe the staff member working with children. Teachers should be meeting on a regular basis with a senior supervisor to review treatment plans and to receive feedback about their work. The teachers, in turn, should offer regular feedback to their classroom assistants about their work.

Unless we are supervised, we tend to repeat the same mistake again and again. Even an experienced, highly skilled person can fall into bad habits or drift from the original training protocol. We can all benefit from feedback. That holds true for you as a parent working with your child as well. Be certain to ask for periodic feedback on your teaching skills from your home support staff member, your child's teacher, or someone else who is knowledgeable.

Feedback should be given in an open and constructive fashion. There is an art to helping people grow in their skills. An important aspect of that art is creating an atmosphere in which the person being supervised feels respected and valued for what she has achieved and challenged to continue to grow. Staff members who feel threatened by the supervision process are less likely to be open to learning and trying new methods and more likely to try to avoid their supervisors!

Parents too will seek more feedback when they feel comfortable with the people offering it. This is a difficult variable to assess, but an important one. Use your intuitive feel to guide how comfortable you might be getting feedback from these professionals. Watch how they interact with the children, with each other, and with you.

Are Staff Up-to-Date on Teaching Methods?

Behavioral teaching methods for working with children with autism have changed radically in the past fifteen years. A program that relies on methods that were in use ten years ago is seriously out of date today. How does the program you are considering ensure that teachers and other staff are able to keep current on teaching methods? One approach is through in-service training, in which an in-house expert or a consultant provides training at the school for staff. Another approach is to send staff to professional conferences on the treatment of autism. There are many conferences every year at which experts on autism spectrum disorders discuss current teaching methods. Staff should be encouraged to attend these meetings and to transfer the skills to their own work. The program should also provide staff with access to current journals and books about teaching methods.

Are Staff and Children "On Target" Most of the Time?

Refer to a copy of the class schedule while you are observing. Are staff members following the teaching programs? Are they adhering to the classroom schedule? Is most of the time spent in active teaching?

Teachers should organize materials ahead of time and be familiar with a child's programs. Minimal time should be spent between programs. Teachers should not be surfing the Internet, chatting with one another, drinking coffee, and so forth. Their task is to be focused on the children. This is not to suggest that there should be no moments of conversation, or that things

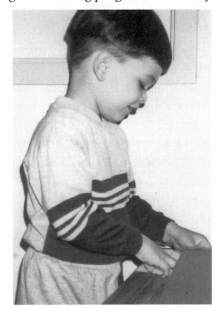

do not sometimes get off schedule. Children are unpredictable, and sometimes flexibility is necessary to meet their needs. However, for most of the teaching day, staff should be on schedule and on task. An excess of down time suggests a failure to be properly organized.

Who Is Responsible?

Does the program have a clear chain of command? Do you know who works with the children? Who supervises that individual? Who is the administrator who runs the program? Can you have access to that administrator if you need to? It should be clear to parents and staff alike who is in charge. In observing a program, you can determine whether there is a clear chain of command by asking staff questions about their supervision experience. For example, ask a teacher, "Who is your supervisor"? or "How often does your supervisor stop by to observe your classroom?"

Selecting the Program for Your Child: High Quality ABA Instruction

The Nature of ABA

There has never been a more hopeful or more confusing time to be a consumer of interventions for autism spectrum disorders. There are a variety of approaches, all of which claim success. Few have data. ABA is the exception to this, with large quantities of data proving its effectiveness for young people with ASD. Choosing ABA can be a lonely choice, even today, as many will question whether it is the best path to take. Parents may be made to feel cruel or unfeeling about choosing a "harsh" or "less humane" approach. Others will criticize parents for choosing a method that is not entirely natural, or will say that social skills will be inadequately addressed. These criticisms are based on misinformation about the nature of ABA, but that doesn't make it easier for parents.

Even when parents have solidly decided upon ABA as their intervention choice, they may encounter confusion about ABA, even within the ABA world. Parents will hear mixed messages about everything from teaching strategies to behavior management. They may attend workshops that criticize discrete trial instruction, emphasizing the use of naturalistic strategies instead. They may hear about the need to teach language through a verbal behavior approach. They may hear about pivotal skills or incidental teaching, which both seek to build skills through more naturalistic methods. They may hear about the need to use punishment to reduce behaviors, or the need to avoid punishment altogether. They may hear about teaching in blocks of repetitive trials, or may be told to avoid doing that entirely. They may hear about the need to collect data on every teaching opportunity, or may be told it is fine to take data on just some instructional opportunities. Even for professionals in the field, the array of choices and the strong opinions can by dizzying. For a consumer, it can feel downright impossible to navigate.

Table 6-2 lists the most important elements of a quality, state-of-the-art program in ABA. We hope it helps to clarify the field's current level of knowledge about what helps learners with autism spectrum disorders most. Of course, our understanding of autism is continually evolving, and this list will evolve with the field over time. Others may have varying opinions about this list, but we believe it is grounded in both empirical validation and philosophical rationale.

Each element on the list is discussed in more detail in the sections below.

Teaching Strategies

Task Interspersal

Until relatively recently, children with autism were taught in blocks of trials, in which the same instruction was repeated over and over again. For example, if the child was learning to touch different body parts, the instructor would say "touch head" ten times in a row. The rationale for this strategy was that children with ASD require multiple opportunities to learn new skills. This

---

Table 6-2 | Important Instructional Elements of
an ABA Program

Teaching Strategies
- Do they utilize task interspersal (mixing new targets with mastered material rather than doing blocks of repetitive trials)?
- Do they teach using errorless procedures?
- Do they use naturalistic ABA teaching methods such as Incidental Teaching, Pivotal Response Training, or Natural Environment Training?
- Do they use methods to increase speed of response (in addition to accuracy of response)?
- Do they address all areas of the curriculum, including social and play skills?

Behavior Management
- Do they use functional behavior assessment (FBA) and functional analysis procedures in determining why a behavior is occurring?
- Do they focus on the use of antecedent strategies to prevent behavior problems?
- Do they focus on the development of appropriate replacement skills that can serve the same function as the problem behavior?
- Do they adhere to the philosophy of and use the techniques associated with Positive Behavioral Supports?

---

is true, but we now know that it is better not to repeat the same instructions over and over again. Whether we are teaching within discrete trials or within a more naturalistic approach, we now avoid repetitive instructions.

To facilitate learning, it is better to mix new tasks with old, mastered material. In this way, we mix easy and hard skills. There are several advantages to this approach, which is often called "task interspersal" or simply "interspersal" (e.g., Dunlap, 1984; Winterling, Dunlap, & O'Neill, 1987). First, students experience less frustration, since they receive more reinforcement than they would if they were doing hard tasks all the time. Second, they can build momentum with responding to easy tasks, and that makes it easier to get harder tasks correct. Perhaps most importantly, it prevents the child from simply responding automatically, based on her expectation that all trials will be alike.

With interspersal, the child must listen to each instruction, as she cannot predict what the next question will be. This makes the instructional time much more similar to "real life," as we cannot predict what questions we will be asked on a moment to moment basis. Interspersal prepares students better for the unpredictable interactions and lessons they are likely to have in all of their future educational settings and social interactions.

Errorless Learning

Another relatively recent change in the use of ABA methods with children with ASD is in how we handle errors in response. In the past, we sometimes allowed learners to make mistakes several times before we prompted them to give the correct answer. The problem is that children on the autism spectrum have a tendency to repeat errors. (Actually, we all have that tendency, but individuals with autism seem to have an extra vulnerability.) Repeated error patterns can sometimes be difficult to fix. Now, we focus on teaching in an *errorless* way (e.g., Etzel & LeBlanc, 1979; Lancioni & Smeets, 1986; Touchette & Howard, 1984).

Errorless learning focuses on the prevention and interruption of errors. We try to prevent errors in new tasks by prompting students with physical or verbal help. We offer a great deal of assistance for new tasks, to ensure that children get the response correct. (This is sometimes called a "most to least" prompt hierarchy, indicating we give the most help for the newest tasks, and we reduce our help as learning takes place.)

We also try to interrupt errors if they start to occur, preventing the individual from completing an incorrect response. For example, if we are working on a labeling program and we ask the child to touch a cup, and she begins to touch a brush, we would take her hand in mid air (before she touched the wrong object), and guide it to the correct object. When errors do happen, we generally correct them, giving the child information about what would have been the correct response. This is done in a neutral tone of voice and never contains any elements of punishment, such as a reprimand. It should also be accompanied by a correction procedure, to help the child understand what was expected of her (e.g., the instructor takes the child's hand, places it on her head, and says, "This is touching head.") All of these strategies help to reduce the likelihood that repeated errors will happen, or that error patterns will develop.

Use of Naturalistic Teaching Strategies

Many people associate ABA with Discrete Trial Instruction (DTI; also called Discrete Trial Training, DTT). DTI is a sequenced form of instruction, designed to be a single moment of teaching a very specific skill. DTI is very focused on the abc's of instruction: **a**ntecedents (i.e., the instruction given), **b**ehavior (i.e., what the child does in response to the instruction), and **c**onsequences (i.e., how the teacher rewards a correct response or handles an error).

DTI is a very clear and comprehensible teaching approach for individuals on the autism spectrum, as it helps them to figure out the most important aspects of the teaching situation and rewards them for correct responses.

DTI was the primary instructional methodology used with students with autism for many years. There is a tremendous amount of published literature documenting its effectiveness in teaching a broad array of skills. It is extremely useful in teaching children to respond to instructions. (This is a major bonus, as many learners with autism ignore social overtures and instructions without such training.) Furthermore, DTI is effective in teaching skills that children find difficult or that are not intrinsically motivating to students.

DTI is not very effective in building initiation skills, however. Students taught only with DTI may learn to respond, but not to initiate. They may be somewhat passive in getting their needs met, and may lack survival skills in less staff-intensive settings. For example, a child who waits for an adult to notice that she needs a pencil or a spoon may be overlooked in a busy classroom environment, and may not get the attention (and the items) she needs to fully participate. Naturalistic strategies help to balance this focus on responsivity with a focus on initiation. The combination of DTI and the naturalistic strategies helps to ensure comprehensive development of skills. DTI is still a very useful and much-needed approach to developing skills in children on the autism spectrum, but must be balanced with naturalistic strategies to ensure development of all important skills.

There are several naturalistic strategies within ABA. All of them emphasize initiation skills and focus on the child's interests. This is in contrast to DTI, which is a more formal instructional approach that is teacher-led and focused on responsiveness.

Incidental Teaching

Incidental Teaching was the first of the naturalistic ABA strategies to be developed (e.g., Hart & Risley, 1982). It has evolved over the years, and can be used to teach a wide variety of skills such as conversational skills, self-help skills, and requesting (Fenske, Krantz, & McClannahan, 2001). Incidental Teaching has been defined as a procedure "used to get elaborated language by waiting for another person to initiate conversation about a topic and then responding in ways that get more language from that person" (Hart & Risley, 1982, p. 5). In contrast to DTI, Incidental Teaching capitalizes *on an interest of the child and on the child's initiation.* Incidental teaching emphasizes *structuring the environment to increase learner initiation.* Teachers might place very highly desired items on high shelves or in containers that are difficult to open, thereby creating opportunities for children to initiate requests.

Another theme in Incidental Teaching is the *elaboration* of the child's response. The teacher tries to pull more language from her when she does make a request. For example, if the child wants bubbles high on a shelf and points to them, saying, "buh," the teacher might request the whole word, "say bubbles." When the child says "bubbles" (offering the more elaborate request), she gets access to the bubbles.

Incidental Teaching is often conceptualized as building initiation skills, which it is highly successful in doing. However, it is often also implemented on a broader level. It can be used to build conversational skills, as well as a wide variety of language and other skills (Fenske, Krantz, & McClannahan, 2001). However it is applied, Incidental Teaching always places an emphasis on the child's interests and initiation, as well as on elaboration. It is a highly useful and versatile teaching strategy, which has been documented as widely effective (Farmer-Dougan, 1994; McGee, Almeida, Sulzer-Azaroff, & Feldman, 1992; McGee, Krantz, & McClannahan, 1985; McGee, Krantz, & McClannahan, 1986).

See Table 6-3 for a description of how Incidental Teaching and Discrete Trial Instruction differ.

Other Naturalistic Strategies

There are several other naturalistic strategies within applied behavior analysis that have been developed since the late 1980s to early 1990s. They all, like incidental teaching, focus on increasing initiation skills. In addition, like incidental teaching, they all focus on the learner's interests. The Natural Language Paradigm and Pivotal Response Train-

Table 6-3 | Comparison of DTI and Incidental Teaching

	Discrete Trial Instruction	Incidental Teaching & Naturalistic ABA Instruction
Who initiates learning opportunity?	Instructor	Student
Where does it occur?	Structured setting	Natural setting
Is it planned?	Definitely	To varying extents
Does it involve repetition?	Yes	Sometimes
What is the nature of the reward?	Extrinsic Rewards (unrelated to the task or activity, e.g, pieces of food; tokens)	Natural Rewards (i.e., related to the task or activity, such as getting to push the truck down the ramp when working on prepositions with a toy garage)

ing (e.g., R. L. Koegel & L. K. Koegel, 2005; R. L. Koegel, L. K. Koegel & A. Surrat, 1992; R. L. Koegel, M. C. O'Dell, & L. K. Koegel, 1987) emphasize teaching with items and activities that are of interest to the child. They also emphasize following the child's lead in choosing materials and targets of instruction. For example, if the child were very interested in cars and ramps, instructors might choose to work on "up" and "down" while playing with a car and a toy garage ramp. Naturalistic teaching sessions are informal, and do not provide the same level of repetition that discrete trial sessions offer. Rewards are natural and are related to the task. For example, a child is reinforced by sending the car down the ramp rather than by getting a gummy bear.

Pivotal Response Training (PRT). Pivotal Response Training (R. L. Koegel & L. K. Koegel, 2005) also focuses on the development of skills that are *pivotal* for children. Pivotal skills are applicable in a wide variety of contexts and activities, and are of central importance in a variety of academic and social tasks. Examples include complying with requests and requesting skills. Two behaviors that are emphasized as essential are: 1) motivation and 2) being able to respond to multiple cues. In fact, difficulties in these areas are perhaps the most incapacitating deficits children with autism spectrum disorders may have.

An unmotivated student does not engage in learning or perform well, may not demonstrate skills on request, and will be lackadaisical in any responses she does make. When motivation is ensured, students respond quickly, correctly, and with *positive affect* (e.g., enthusiasm, excitement). PRT ensures that a student is motivated and engaged in learning.

A student who cannot attend to multiple cues will be para-lyzed in the natural environment, where there are myriad cues for a multitude of tasks. For example, at school cues for different types of behaviors can include worksheet instructions, class schedule, verbal directions, class rules, word boards, etc. When students cannot navigate such environments or interpret such cues, they are unable to function without support. In contrast, students who can respond to multiple cues are more independent. PRT can assist children in interpreting multiple cues and in figuring out which cues are relevant at which times and for which activities.

Other aspects central to PRT are child choice and initiation. That is, the teacher tends to follow the child's lead in deciding what to work on during any given teaching session.

Natural Environment Training (NET). Another natu-ralistic ABA strategy that has received a great deal of attention in recent years is Natural Environment Training (Sundberg & Parting-ton, 1998). NET contains many of the themes and elements of the other naturalistic strategies we have discussed, including a focus on allowing the child's interests to guide instruction, an emphasis on the development of initiation skills, and the use of natural environ-ments and naturally occurring events as settings and opportuni-ties for instruction. NET also adds to these themes the use of the Verbal Behavior language classification system to teach language.

This classification system was developed by B. F. Skinner, and is described in his book *Verbal Behavior* (1957).

Skinner outlined a variety of *functions* of language, several of which are highly relevant to teaching children with ASD. See Table 6-4 for a description of the most relevant of Skinner's verbal *operants* (descriptions of the functions of language.)

Table 6-4 | Skinner's Verbal Operants

Mand—A request
Tact—Labelling
Intraverbal—A conversational exchange
Echoic—Verbal imitation

Children with autism have deficits using language for many of these functions. They have difficulty requesting, labeling, imitating, and carrying on a conversation. Furthermore, when we target one of these problem areas, we often get improvement in only that area. In other words, we may teach a child to expressively *label* objects (e.g., juice), and she may learn to *identify* the object on request. Nevertheless, she may not be able to *request* that same object, even when she very much wants or needs it. For example, she may not request juice even when she is thirsty. Mark Sundberg and James Partington (1998) make the point that we must develop specific teaching programs for each function of language to ensure that the child develops the ability to communicate in a comprehensive way. See Table 6-5 for examples of each verbal operant.

Partington and Sundberg (1998) have developed a comprehensive assessment and curricular planning package which uses the VB classification system for teaching the core expressive language skills. This is an excellent resource. Their emphases on the use of skills in the natural environment and in a generalized context make it a very relevant and useful way to measure real progress.

Even these developers of NET, however, have emphasized the need for both DTI and NET in meeting the comprehensive needs

Table 6-5 | Examples of Verbal Operants

MAND

Essential features:

* Request
* Can be vocal or nonvocal

Examples:

* Saying, "Mama, pretend you are a cow."
* Reaching for a xylophone
* Looking at a desired cookie
* Leading a parent to the juice bottle
* Saying, "I want cookie please."

TACT

Essential features:

* Labeling an aspect of the environment
* Often is combined with other operants (e.g., mand plus tact)

Examples:

* Saying "lights" when seeing a display of holiday lights
* Saying "popcorn" when smelling popcorn
* Saying "airplane" and pointing to a plane in the sky

INTRAVERBAL

Essential features:

* To and fro conversational exchange
* Talking about things not physically present or currently experienced
* Sometimes combined with other operants when discussing things present (e.g., intraverbal plus tact)

Examples:

* A conversation about your weekend
* A conversation about a movie you saw
* A conversation about princesses or superheroes

ECHOIC

Essential features:

* Vocal imitation of sounds or words

Examples:

* Instructor says, "Say cookie." Child says, "Cookie."
* Instructor says, "Say Emily." Child says, "Emily."

of children with autism (Sundberg & Partington, 1999.) NET has many advantages, and may be the best way to build skills in the all-important areas of manding (requesting) and intraverbal skills (conversational language). DTI, however, is still probably the most effective way to build skills in certain curricular areas such as receptive language (language comprehension) and tacting (expressive labeling.) Furthermore, as mentioned earlier, DTI is often the best choice for teaching skills in areas in which the child does not have an intrinsic interest. This is because in DTI, the child is rewarded for each response she makes with a reinforcer that is motivating to her. If a child is not intrinsically interested in the material or object of the lesson, it will be difficult to reinforce her with that object or activity (which is the approach used in NET). An unrelated reward would be a more effective motivator for a task that is not compellingly interesting or highly preferred.

In other words, if your child needs to learn many expressive language skills, but struggles with articulation, it may be helpful for you to find a program that incorporates both DTI—to build precision in vocal imitation—and naturalistic strategies—to develop reciprocal (back-and-forth) communication.

The Bottom Line

The most important aspect of teaching strategies is the recognition that children with autism spectrum disorders need a combination of both naturalistic and formal teaching strategies. Both DTI and the naturalistic strategies are highly effective in building skills. However, they are best suited to the development of *different* skills. For comprehensive program-

ming, you want to select a program that utilizes both types of ABA instruction. For example:

If your child needs to learn many expressive language skills, it may be helpful for you to find a program that uses the NET approach or incidental teaching to target initiation, requesting, and conversational skills, and DTI to build vocal imitation, receptive language, and labeling skills. On the other hand, if it is difficult to motivate your child to engage in any social interaction and she has deficits in many areas of the curriculum, it may be helpful for you to find a program that uses naturalistic strategies to increase rapport and engagement with the instructor and DTI to build core foundation skills in multiple areas.

Other Issues

Parents are sometimes also confused about a few other "hot topics" in applied behavior analysis. At the time of this writing, two of the major hot topics include fluency and data collection.

Rate-building for Fluency

Recently, there has been an increased emphasis on ensuring that skills are taught to "fluency" (e.g., Weiss, 2001). Carl Binder has described fluency as "the fluid combination of accuracy plus speed" (Binder, 1996, p.164). Skills that are fluent are easy for the person to demonstrate, and have an automatic, freely flowing quality.

Historically, within ABA intervention for autism, we have focused mostly on accuracy and less on speed. Students were considered to have mastered skills as long as they could demonstrate the skill on a certain percentage of opportunities (such as 80 or 90 percent of the time). Recently, however, we have increased our sensitivity to fluency levels. In other words, can your child do this skill quickly? Can he or she do it as quickly as typical peers?

One reason for this interest in fluency is that we have become aware of how lags in response time (sometimes called *latency to response*) can result in missed social opportunities. For example, if a peer in at school greets a classmate with ASD and does not get a response for seven or eight seconds, the chance of a social connection falls precipitously. Eight seconds is a long time for a five- or six-year-old. Many peers will be gone when the response does come. This is why accuracy alone may be inadequate. Although the child did eventually answer, it was not at a speed that was meaningful or successful in a social context. Similarly, if a teacher calls on a child in circle time, but has to wait ten seconds for a reply, the child may miss out on the opportunity to participate. Often, in this situation, a teacher simply needs to move on or risk losing the attention of the entire class.

There are several ways to address fluency in ABA-based programs for children with ASD. First, we pay attention to pacing in instructional programming. The goal is to maximize the number of opportunities to learn. In rate-building, the teacher tries to get as many responses as possible from the child within a given amount of time. This helps to provide sufficient practice of the skill. Second, we pay attention to the issue of lag in response time, such as in response to greetings. Sometimes, a program may do rate-building with timed practice sessions. This is an excellent way to speed up responding. This is another sub-area of ABA, called Precision Teaching. Data are sparse on the use of rate building with children with ASD, but research is increasing (e.g., Fabrizio & Moors, 2003).

Sometimes instructors attempt to increase a child's learning opportunities and build speed of response within the contexts of the typical programming. For example, a teacher may present the child with pictures to label more rapidly or may simply begin tracking how long it takes her to respond to questions (without doing timed practices as described above). Either way, working on response speed can enhance your child's success in the real world.

In general, students respond very positively to rate-building, in part because of all the coaching and reinforcement that accompanies it. Occasionally, a child may become anxious or frustrated during rate-building. This is almost always because reinforcement needs to be increased, task expectations need to be adjusted, or prerequisite skills need to mastered. Attention to the child's response to instruction is a part of all good ABA practice, including rate-building.

Data Collection

Another "hot topic" is data collection. Some ABA programs may take trial by trial data, creating a record of each learning opportunity. Other programs may take data periodically by probing the skill through a variety of systematic strategies. There is not enough research comparing these two approaches yet, and each has merits, advantages, and disadvantages. The important thing for you as a consumer is to choose a program that collects objective data on a frequent basis, and that uses those data to make decisions about teaching.

A quality program that uses ABA for educating children with autism will keep careful records of the children's progress. Sometimes these records may be what we call "trial by trial data." Trial by trial recordkeeping involves recording whether each response by a child was correct, and may involve recording whether or not she needed help (a prompt) to complete a task. For example, if the teacher instructs your child to "do this" ten times, she may record a plus for each time your child responds correctly, and a minus for each time she responds incorrectly, and at the end of the session will know what percentage of trials your child completed correctly. (Keep in mind that these trials would not be done as a block, but would be interspersed with mastered tasks, as we discussed earlier.) Advantages of the trial by trial data collection are that it is the most accountable data collection system, and that it allows for calculation of the number of trials required for mastery.

Another method of record keeping is to collect "probes" on a child's performance. Rather than taking the time to make a record of performance after each response, the teacher sets aside a block of time to record progress. For example, probes may be conducted once or twice a day or once every several days. When done once or twice a day, first trial probes are often used. In this situation, the teacher records performance on the skill the very first time the child is asked to do it in the teaching session. Often, there are two probes per day, one in the morning teaching session and one in the afternoon teaching session. Alternately, a teacher might collect data on Friday afternoon on the several programs she is using with a child. She may take first trial probe data or she may record performance on several instances of the behavior. However, this would be a sample of performance for the week, as daily data was not taken.

Whether probes are done daily, several times a week, or weekly, they are done on a schedule to ensure regular data collection. However, if the teacher believes your child has mastered a program sooner, she could do a probe at any time she wished.

A quality program will evaluate data daily, in an effort to maximize the effectiveness of instruction. When you are evaluating programs, staff should be willing to explain to you how often they collect data and how parents are granted access to their child's data.

The Goals of ABA

Many people have misconceptions about what ABA targets, believing that teachers who use ABA methods can target cognitive or language skills, but not social skills. This is a misconception that stems from people equating DTI with ABA, and not understanding how instructors use naturalistic strategies in concert with DTI to build skills across curricular areas. In reality, ABA is a comprehensive intervention that focuses on all deficits that are relevant for a particular child.

ABA's strengths include:

1. the definition of target skills,
2. the clear and precise delineation of teaching methods, and
3. the use of objective data to determine when skills have been mastered and to guide adjustments in instruction.

All of these strengths can be used to guide programming in the elusive area of social skills instruction, just as they do in other domains. In recent years, ABA has increased its attention to teach-

ing core social skills such as joint attention, reciprocal conversation, perspective taking, and problem solving. We discuss the use of ABA in *Reaching Out, Joining In,* our book on teaching social skills to children on the autism spectrum (Weiss & Harris, 2001).

To make sure that any program you are considering understands the importance of teaching social skills, ask about how social skills are assessed and about the instructional approaches used to build social skills. You can also ask whether social skills are ever taught in a group lesson.

Behavior Management

How challenging behavior is handled during ABA instruction has changed radically since behavior modification was first used in teaching children with autism spectrum disorders. In the past, the focus was simply on reducing behavior that interfered with learning or was otherwise disruptive or dangerous. Now, the focus is on understanding behavior and preventing its occurrence (O'Neill et al., 1992).

We now know that behavior does not occur in a vacuum, but happens because it serves a function for the individual. A student may tear up a worksheet to get out of doing a task that is too difficult. A student may turn over her desk because it will instantly bring over the teacher, and she may have no other way to request that level of quick attention. Once we understand *why* a behavior occurs, we can develop strategies to prevent the behavior. These strategies, often called *antecedent strategies* because they precede and prevent the behavior from happening, are highly effective. A student who is tearing up worksheets that are too difficult can be given simpler work. She may be given word matching sheets instead of spelling tasks. Or, she may be asked to do the difficult worksheets for briefer periods of time, or in combination with other, more highly preferred tasks. All of these strategies might help the student to cope more effectively with the demands, without resorting to the challenging behavior. In this way, the antecedent strategies are preventive.

Furthermore, we can teach alternate or replacement behaviors that serve the same function as the challenging behavior. The child who tears up the worksheet can be taught to request help or a break. The child who turns over her desk can be taught to solicit teacher attention in an appropriate way, such as by raising her hand. Raising her hand is a replacement behavior; it replaces turning over her desk, while serving the same function of gaining teacher attention.

The use of these approaches has resulted in a radically different approach to reducing challenging behaviors. It is no longer at all common to need to use punishment procedures (e.g., loud reprimands) in treating challenging behaviors. You should be skeptical of any program that relies on punishment to address challenging behaviors except in very rare situations when the alternatives have been exhausted.

You will want to know that the program you select for your child is up-to-date in the use of behavioral assessment and intervention techniques. Specifically, you will want your child in a program that:

1. does comprehensive functional assessments of challenging behaviors,

2. uses antecedent strategies,
3. teaches replacement skills, and
4. uses positive behavioral supports.

Functional Assessment Procedures to Determine Function of Behavior

While nearly all programs for students with special needs now use functional assessment or functional analysis procedures, there is wide variability in which methods are used and in how those methods are used. You should look for a program that has a behavior analyst or a behavioral psychologist who knows how to do a formal functional behavior assessment (FBA).

An FBA is a systematic procedure for determining the function of a child's behavior (for example, to get attention, to escape from demands, or to obtain an object or get access to an activity). It involves gathering information from everyone (including the child and parent) who may have knowledge of the behavior, and direct observation of the child to see what precedes the behavior, what the behavior really involves, and what she "gets" from the behavior. Through repeated direct observations, patterns in behavioral function are then identified.

If the program does use FBAs, find out whether they use direct observational measures as part of their assessments (vs. questionnaires or interviews). Direct observational measures are much better in identifying the functions of behaviors than are questionnaires.

If your child's program uses FBAs effectively, your child will be more likely to have a behavior reduction plan that will work. For a very thorough explanation of how FBAs should be conducted, you may want to read *Functional Behavior Assessments for People with Autism: Making Sense of Seemingly Senseless Behavior* (Glasberg, 2005).

Focus on Antecedent Strategies

Although FBAs are very useful tools in dealing with existing behavior challenges, you want to be sure that your child's behaviors are managed primarily through *prevention*. Once your child is well understood by staff, they can ensure that the likelihood of behavioral difficulties is diminished through a variety of preventive tactics. Recall that these strategies are called antecedent strategies, because they come *before* the target behavior. Many behavioral challenges can be prevented, through modifications of the environment or materials, or through changes in the curriculum.

The use of antecedent strategies goes hand in hand with functional behavior assessment. For example, we can prevent an escape-motivated behavior by modifying the curriculum to reduce difficulty, by mixing hard and easy tasks, and by using preferred materials. See Table 6-6 on the next page for a description of commonly used and effective antecedent strategies that match particular functions of behavior. You want to be sure that any program you consider uses antecedent strategies as a primary strategy to manage challenging behaviors.

Focus on the Development of Replacement Skills

An element essential to the comprehensive treatment of challenging behavior is the identification of, and instruction in, replacement skills. Students need to be taught effective ways to communicate their messages and to get their needs met. We need to help them develop alternate behaviors that are more adaptive, but which still help them to communicate their needs. We must also ensure that the response we teach works at least as well as the challenging behavior worked. In other words, we must make sure that a request for a break gives immediate access to a break, or that a request for attention results in fast attending by a teacher. A list of common replacement skills is contained in Table 6-7 on page 161.

You want to be sure that any program you consider focuses on the development of replacement skills that match the function of a challenging behavior. In this way, you can be assured that your child will learn adaptive ways to communicate her needs and to get them met.

> ### Table 6-6 | Common Antecedent Strategies (Based on Function)
>
> **Attention-motivated behavior**
> - Make the environment rich in attention
> - Provide attention noncontingently (e.g., not in response to any particular behavior, on a schedule)
> - Increase opportunities for appropriate social interaction
>
> **Escape-motivated behavior**
> - Provide frequent breaks
> - Intersperse mastered tasks with novel material to reduce frustration
> - Remediation: step back to address deficits in simpler tasks
> - Provide choices of tasks, task order, task location, etc.
>
> **Tangible-motivated behavior**
> *(Behaviors stemming from a desire for some specific item)*
> - Give noncontingent access to preferred items (e.g., provide access to preferred toys on a schedule to help prevent frustration with long delays in being allowed to play with desired toys)
> - Focus on mand training so the child can request desired items
>
> **Behavior maintained by automatic reinforcement**
> *(Behaviors such as rocking or hand flapping that may provide sensory feedback)*
> - Introduce items that compete with the behavior (e.g., toys with similar visual, auditory, or tactile feedback)
> - Provide access noncontingently to items and activities serving this function (give regular access to toys that provide desired sensory input)

Positive Behavioral Supports

Much of what we have discussed in this section overlaps considerably with the concept of positive behavioral supports. PBS has evolved from the basic concepts and principles of ABA, and (like ABA) also emphasizes the prevention of challenging behaviors, the use of antecedent strategies to accommodate the needs of an individual, and respect for the dignity of each person we serve.

Table 6-7 | Common Replacement Skills
(Based on Function)

Attention-motivated behavior
- Teach requesting attention from teacher
- Teach joint attention skills
- Teach requesting attention from peers

Escape-motivated behavior
- Teach requesting a break
- Teach choice making skills

Tangible-motivated behavior
- Teach manding (via speech, sign, PECS, etc.)
- Build skills in using an effective communication system

Behavior maintained by automatic reinforcement
- Teach requests for items that compete with the behavior
  (e.g., a Lite Brite toy to replace visually fixating on
  classroom lights)

There is some debate in the field about how to understand the relationship between ABA and PBS, and it is beyond the scope of this chapter to delve into this relationship in great detail. What is important to know is that the philosophy of PBS is entirely compatible with (and many say synonymous with) other schools of thought and approaches within ABA.

In a program that uses positive behavioral supports, staff work to minimize and prevent behavior problems with a wide array of measures. This includes attention to environmental, social, and task characteristics. For example, they try to limit frustration by giving children breaks when they look like they need one, or by making sure they have frequent opportunities to be rewarded. (This is largely synonymous with antecedent strategies discussed earlier.) And if problem behaviors do occur, PBS interventionists look at the behavior as being a communication of some kind. (Again, this is part of good ABA practice, as discussed earlier in this chapter as part of ABA practice.) In general, a program that uses PBS completely avoids the use of punishment. (Again, as discussed earlier, there has been a dramatic reduction in the need for and use of punishment within ABA.)

You want to be sure that any program you consider adheres to the philosophical themes of PBS and upholds these values.

In Sum

You need to ask hard questions when you select a program for your child. Although no program is perfect, there are some excellent resources available for the education of children with autism. Visit each program with a list of items that you want to observe. As you watch the classroom in action, you may find the answers to some of your questions. You can learn other information during an interview with a senior administrator. Don't feel shy about asking what you need to know. Feel free to bring a list of questions with you, so you can check to see whether you have addressed all your areas of concern. You want to be sure that the program is a good fit for your child, and you want to have as much information as possible to help you make the best choice for him or her. It may be useful to also speak with other parents about their impressions and experiences, although some parents find that this confuses them further. Just keep in mind that any information gathered must be filtered through the lens of your child, and his or her very unique characteristics and needs.

Parents Speak

My son's teacher and her assistants are very caring and dedicated individuals. We are all working together to see that he reaches his full potential. It is so important that everyone involved is working toward a common goal. All lines of communication should be open between home and school. In addition to school, my son still has twelve hours of home therapy a week and my home coordinator is also in touch with his teacher. They work together to try to solve any existing problems. I too am in daily contact with my son's teacher. I know the programs he is working on and I carry it all out at home whenever possible. What's taught at school must be done at home to be successful.

∾

We visited six different programs before Kimmy started school. Mostly, I just watched whenever we went to observe. We saw plenty of programs who all said they were doing the same things, but they looked very different to us in practice. One program used a lot of punishment. We saw one kid being made to stand up and sit down over and over again, and he looked totally miserable. At other programs, teachers and kids looked happy to be there, and seemed very positive. Those things mattered to us in the end. We wanted our daughter to be having fun at school, especially considering how many hours she would be there.

∾

Be sure to tell other parents to take a list of questions with them. I always got kind of nervous when we were in the schools and it helped to have my list so I knew I wouldn't forget any-thing. Nobody seemed to mind. I liked feeling free to call back if we did have questions.

∾

I found it really hard to figure out what kind of ABA I wanted, and even whether what I wanted was ABA. I met other parents who were trying just as hard as I was to get (what I thought was) the opposite of what I wanted (they wanted DTI and I wanted VB). Now I can see just how confused I was, and I don't know how I ever made the right choice given how misinformed

I really was. I guess there was a lot of luck or a guardian angel involved. Anyway, my advice to parents is not to get sucked into the current debates. Try to educate yourself the best you can, and try to find reasonable and balanced professionals to bounce questions off of. Stay focused on your kid. The bottom line was that Henry needed help in initiating, as he was horribly passive, just waiting for life to happen to him. I now know he needed something that would build initiation skills, but that could have happened a lot of different ways....

References

Binder, C. (1996). Behavioral fluency: Evolution of a new paradigm. *The Behavior Analyst, 19*, 163-197.

Dunlap, G. (1984). The influence of task variation and maintenance tasks on the learning of autistic children. *Journal of Experimental Child Psychology, 37*, 41-64.

Etzel, B. C. & LeBlanc, J. M. (1979). The simplest treatment alternative: The law of parsimony applied to choosing appropriate instructional control and errorless learning procedures for the difficult-to-teach child. *Journal of Autism and Developmental Disorders, 9*, 361-382.

Fabrizio, M. A. & Moors, A. L. (2003). Evaluating mastery: Measuring instructional outcomes for children with autism. *European Journal of Behavior Analysis, 4*, 23-36.

Farmer-Dougan, V. (1994). Increasing requests by adults with developmental disabilities using incidental teaching by peers. *Journal of Applied Behavior Analysis, 27*, 533-544.

Fenske, E. C., Krantz, P. J., & McClannahan, L. E. (2001). Incidental teaching: A not-so-discrete-trial teaching procedure. In C. Maurice, G. Green, & R. M. Foxx (Eds.), *Making a Difference: Behavioral Intervention for Autism*. Austin, Texas: Pro-Ed.

Glasberg, B. (2006). *Functional behavior assessment for people with autism: Making sense of seemingly senseless behavior.* Bethesda, MD: Woodbine House.

Hart, B. M., & Risley, T. R. (1982). *How to use incidental teaching for elaborating language*. Austin, TX: Pro-Ed.

Koegel, R. L. & Koegel, L. K. (2005). *Pivotal response treatments for autism*. Baltimore, MD: Brookes Publishing Company.

Koegel, R. L., Koegel, L. K., & Surrat, A. (1992). Language intervention and disruptive behavior in preschool children with autism. *Journal of Autism and Developmental Disorders, 22,* 141-153.

Koegel, R. L. O'Dell, M. C., & Koegel, L. K. (1987). A natural language teaching paradigm for nonverbal autistic children. *Journal of Autism and Developmental Disorders, 17,* 187-200.

Lancioni, G. E., & Smeets, P. M. (1986). Procedures and parameters of errorless discrimination training with developmentally impaired individuals. In N. R. Ellis & N. W. Bray (Eds.), *International Review of Research in Mental Retardation, 14* (pp. 135-164). Orlando, FL: Academic Press.

McGee, G. G., Almeida, M. C., Sulzer-Azaroff, B., & Feldman, R. S. (1992). Promoting reciprocal interactions via peer incidental teaching. *Journal of Applied Behavior Analysis, 25,* 117-126.

McGee, G. G., Krantz, P. J., & McClannahan, L. E. (1985). The facilitative effects of incidental teaching on preposition use by autistic children. *Journal of Applied Behavior Analysis, 18,* 17-31.

McGee, G. G., Krantz, P. J., & McClannahan, L. E. (1986). An extension of incidental teaching procedures to reading instruction for autistic children. *Journal of Applied Behavior Analysis, 19,* 147-157.

Partington, J. W. & Sundberg, M. L. (1998). *The assessment of basic learning and language skills.* Pleasant Hill, CA: Behavior Analysts, Inc.

Skinner, B. F. (1957). *Verbal behavior.* New York: Appleton-Century-Crofts.

Sundberg, M. L. & Partington, J. W. (1998). *Teaching language to children with autism or other developmental disabilities.* Pleasant Hill, CA: Behavior Analysts, Inc.

Sundberg, M. L. & Partington, J. W. (1999). The need for both DT and NE training for children with autism. In P. M. Ghezzi, W. L. Williams, & J. E. Carr (Eds.), *Autism: Behavior Analytic Approaches.* Reno, NV: Context Press.

Terrace, H. (1963). Discrimination learning with and without errors. *Journal of the Experimental Analysis of Behavior, 6,* 1-27.

Touchette, P. E. & Howard, J. (1984). Errorless learning: Reinforcement contingencies and stimulus control transfer in delayed prompting. *Journal of Applied Behavior Analysis, 17,* 175-181.

Weiss, M. J. (2001). Expanding ABA intervention in intensive programs for children with autism: The inclusion of natural environment training and fluency based instruction. *The Behavior Analyst Today, 2,* 182-187.

Weiss, M. J. & Harris, S. L. (2001). *Reaching out, joining in: Teaching social skills to young children with autism*. Bethesda, MD: Woodbine House.

Winterling, V., Dunlap, G., & O'Neill, R. E. (1987). The influence of task variation on the aberrant behaviors of autistic students. *Education and Treatment of Children, 10*, 105-119.

Resources

Autism

Here are two resources you can check that will connect you to many sources of information and support.

Autism Resources
www.autism-resources.com
Through this site, created by John Wobus, you can find the Internet address of nearly every major autism-related site we know of.

Autism Society of America
910 Woodmont Ave., Ste. 650
Bethesda, MD 20814
800-328-8476; 301-657-0869 (fax)
www.autism-society.org
The Autism Society of America has both a fine home page and material they can mail you (via good old snail mail!). You will find lots of information for new parents, membership information, help in finding your local chapter, etc.

Applied Behavior Analysis

Association for Behavior Analysis International
1219 S. Park St.

Kalamazoo, MI 49001
269-492-9310; 269-492-9316
www.abainternational.org

If you become really involved in ABA, you may be interested in the annual meeting of the Association for Behavior Analysis International. Top people in the field assemble there to report on current research. However, unlike the annual convention of the Autism Society of America, which is oriented toward families, this is a meeting for professionals, so expect a lot of debate about the details of research.

Behavior Analyst Certification Board
1705 Metropolitan Blvd., Ste. 102
Tallahassee, FL 32308
www.bacb.com

For help in finding a behavioral consultant or for information on the credentials needed to become certified as a Board Certified Behavior Analyst, visit this website. You can search the online Certificant Registry for consultants in your state or country who are officially certified by the BACB.

Research

To keep abreast of the latest research into autism and its treatment or to get your family involved in a research study, you may want to check out one of these organizations.

Association for Science in Autism Treatment
389 Main St., Ste. 202
Malden, MA 02148
781-397-8943
www.asatonline.org

Autism Speaks
2 Park Ave., 11th Floor

New York, NY 10016
212-252-8584
www.autismspeaks.org

Organization for Autism Research
2000 N. 14th St., Ste. 480
Arlington, VA 22201
703-243-9710
www.researchautism.org

*A note of caution: Anyone can create a web page.
The material you find on the Internet may or may not be accurate.
Although there is a great deal of useful information in cyberspace,
there is also some baloney. Use very good judgment!*

Index

food as, 119-20
for building compliance, 97-98
importance of, 117-18
types of, 8
with DTI, 151
Replication, 37, 41-42
Requesting. *See* Manding
Research
evaluating, 35-42
on Intensive Behavioral
Intervention, 31-35
participating in, 42-43
terms, 36-37
Resistance to instruction, 98
Responses, slow, 152-53
Rett's disorder, xii, 121
Rewards. *See* Reinforcement
Risley, Todd, 9
Sallows, Glen, 34
School-based programs
combining with home-based
services, 84
compared to home- or
center-based programs, 74
distractions and, 80
family involvement in, 77
peers and, 80-81
staff and, 79
support services and, 132
transportation and, 79
School district, persuading to
fund home program, 82-84
Sd
definition of, 105, 106
examples of, 111
Self-stimulation, 160, 161
Sets, of skills, 113
Siblings, 137-38
Single parents, 76
Slow responses, 152-53
Skinner, B.F., 128, 149
Smith, Tristram, 13, 32, 34

Social skills, 103-104, 115, 153, 156
Social workers, 61
Speech-language specialists, 57,
60-61
Summer services, 133
Sundberg, Mark, 11, 149
Supervision, of teachers, 138-40
Tact, 150
Target behavior, 106
Task interspersal, 8, 141-43
Teachers, 57, 59-60. *See also*
Instructors
Teaching program. *See* Curriculum; Program, teaching
Teaching strategies
errorless learning, 143-44
incidental teaching, 145-46
Natural Environment Training,
148-51
naturalistic, 9-11, 144-45
Pivotal Response training, 147-48
task interspersal, 8, 141-43
Tests. *See also* Evaluations
objective vs. subjective, 39-40
Transitions, from one program to
another, 50-51, 133-34
Tutors. *See* Instructors
Vacations, 133
Verbal Behavior classification
system, 148-49
Verbal operants, 149
Volunteers, 72
Walden Preschool, 55
Zalenski, Stanley, 33

About the Authors

Sandra L. Harris, Ph.D., is a Board of Governors Distinguished Service Professor at the Graduate School of Applied and Professional Psychology and the Department of Psychology at Rutgers, The State University of New Jersey. She is the Founder and Executive Director of the Douglass Developmental Disabilities Center at Rutgers, which serves people with autism from toddlers through adults. Dr. Harris is the editor of Woodbine House's *Topics in Autism* series.

Mary Jane Weiss, Ph.D., BCBA, is Research Associate Professor at Rutgers. She is the Director of the Division of Research and Training at the Douglass Developmental Disabilities Center.